James Cusack

Lectures on Music

Staff Notation. Third Edition

James Cusack

Lectures on Music
Staff Notation. Third Edition

ISBN/EAN: 9783337084639

Printed in Europe, USA, Canada, Australia, Japan

Cover: Foto ©Thomas Meinert / pixelio.de

More available books at **www.hansebooks.com**

LECTURES ON MUSIC.

STAFF NOTATION.

By

JAMES CUSACK.

THIRD EDITION.

1899.

2/- net.

London:

THE CITY OF LONDON BOOK DEPÔT,
White Street and Finsbury Street,
Moorfields, E.C.

LONDON:
STRAKER BROTHERS, LTD.,
44-47, BISHOPSGATE WITHOUT, E.C.

PREFACE.

This little book is intended for Students preparing for the examinations of the Education Department, and includes all that is required in Theory of Music, Staff Notation, by Pupil Teachers during their whole course, by Scholarship Candidates, and by Certificate Students of the First and Second Year.

It also contains some interesting matter beyond what is required for the examinations just named, and which renders it a useful text book for students preparing for the Elementary Theory Examinations of the Royal Academy of Music, the Royal College of Music, the Society of Arts, and other similar examinations.

Not being a teacher of **practical** music myself, I am indebted to Mr. W. R. Phillips, Fellow and Member of the Tonic Sol-Fa College, for the chapter on Voice Training, and for the contents of that chapter he is solely responsible.

The rest of the work is composed entirely from the Teaching Notes and Manuscript Lesson Papers which for some years I have used, I may say with success, in teaching both Oral and Correspondence Classes.

J. CUSACK.

DAY TRAINING COLLEGE,
White Street, Moorfields, in the City of London,
1st of October, 1892.

PREFACE TO THE THIRD EDITION.

A SECOND edition of this book having been called for in 1896 it was reprinted with merely a few verbal alterations, and the correction of a few typographical errors.

Another edition being now required, I have taken advantage of the further experience gained in the use of the book and have made some alterations. Chapters III. and VII. in the older editions have each been divided into two separate chapters, as the different parts of the subject matter in each seemed sufficiently distinct to justify that; and while the number of distinct articles remains as in the earlier editions, considerable additions have been made to a few of them, slight additions have been made to some, and slight alterations in many, wherever I found it possible to make the matter clearer, or the explanation fuller, for Correspondence Students, whose interests I have kept constantly in view in the revision of the text. Some additional questions have also been added.

I have to express my sincere thanks to the large number of Teachers through whose favour this book on Staff Notation has acquired such a wide circulation, a circulation all the more remarkable at a time when many would have us believe that everything else must disappear before the Tonic Sol-Fa Notation for elementary students, and when more than three-fourths, even of my own London students, are studying the latter system exclusively.

J. CUSACK.

DAY TRAINING COLLEGE,
  MOORFIELDS, LONDON, E.C.
    13th *November*, 1899.

CONTENTS.

—:o:—

Chapter I.
                                                                                          PAGE

Musical Notes—Alphabetic and Syllabic Names—The Great Staff—Bass Staff—Treble Staff—Middle C—Clefs—Full Score—Short Score—Leger Lines—Pitch .. .. .. 1—17

Chapter II.

Time—Time Names of Notes—Dotted Notes—Rests—Dotted Rests—The Tie—Bar and Bar Lines—Measures—Beats—Value of Bars, and of Single Notes—Various Kinds of Time—Simple and Compound Time—The Metronome—Accent and Syncopation—The Triplet.. .. .. .. 18—45

Chapter III.

The Scale—Tone and Semitone—Tetrachords—Sharps, Flats, and Naturals—The Common Scale—Other Scales—Natural Order of Scale Formation—Key Signatures—How to tell the Key from the Signature, whether Sharps or Flats .. .. .. 46—67

Chapter IV.

Intervals—Kind and Quality of Intervals—How to tell the Kind and Quality of Intervals—How to write Intervals of given Kind and Quality—Augmented and Diminished Intervals—Intervals found in the Major Scale .. .. 68—80

Chapter V.

The Minor Scale—Difference between Major and Minor Scales—Relative Minor Scale—Various Forms of Minor Scale—How to tell the Minor Key from the Signature—Different effects of the Major and Minor Scale—The Tonic Minor—Different forms of the Tonic Minor—Tonic Major—Intervals found in the Minor Scale .. .. 81—103

Chapter VI.

PAGE

The Tonic, Dominant, Sub-Dominant, &c.—Mental effects of these Notes—Modulation—Transition—Principal and Subordinate Keys—Relative or Attendant Keys—Natural and Extraneous Modulation—Laws of Modulation—Transposition from one Key to Another—Compound Intervals—Transposition from one Kind of Time to another—Transcription—Laws of Transcription.. .. .. ..104—123

Chapter VII.

Double Bars—Various Terms and Signs—Grace Notes—List of Terms relating to Pace—List of Terms relating to Expression and Style .. ..124—133

Chapter VIII.

Inversion of Intervals—Two ways of Inverting—Change of Kind on Inversion—Change of Quality on Inversion ..134—135

Chapter IX.

Chords—The Common Chord—The Triad—Intervals in the Triad—Inversion of a Chord—First Inversion—Second Inversion—The Six-Three Chord—The Six-Four Chord—Figuring of Chords—Writing Chords from Figures ..136—142

Chapter X.

Voice Training—Causes of Flattening—Rules for Voice Cultivation—Breathing—Compass of Voices—Classification of Voices—Registers .. ..143—148

QUESTIONS ON THE TEXT .. ..149—192

ALPHABETICAL INDEX .. ..193—196

CUSACK'S
LECTURES ON MUSIC.

CHAPTER I.

Notes, Staves, Leger Lines, Clefs.

1. Music is produced by a succession or repetition of sounds, with or without alternations of silence, arranged so as to give us pleasure through the sense of hearing.

2. If in the succession we hear only one sound at any one time, we call the music **Melody**, but if we hear a suitable combination of two or more sounds at one time, then we call it **Harmony**.

3. Some sounds only are musical: some sounds instead of pleasure, give us great annoyance, these we call **Noise**.

4. A complete study of the nature and production of musical sounds, and of the relation of musical sounds to one another, belongs to the science subject **Sound**, and will not be attempted here.

5. Musical sounds are produced by the human voice and by the various kinds of musical instruments.

6. Musical sounds are of various kinds. There is the **low, deep, grave** sound, as in the **bass** voice of a man. There is the **shrill, clear, acute** sound, as in the treble voices of women and children, and there are various grades between these two.

7. The great difficulty in music is, how to indicate on paper the various musical sounds, and to read the sounds that have been indicated by certain **characters**.

8. The characters used to represent musical sounds are called **Notes**, just as the characters used to represent the sounds used in reading are called **Letters**, or as the characters used to represent numbers are called **Figures**. Musical sounds themselves are also spoken of as Notes.

9. There should be no more trouble in learning to read music than in learning to read poetry, or prose, or in learning to read numbers, if the same pains will be taken in the early stages to familiarise the learner with the musical sound and its representative note at the same time, and to exercise his powers of discrimination as soon as he has learned a second or a third musical sound, by requiring him frequently to distinguish the one from the other, to produce each one as called for, and to name those produced for him, just as a child is exercised in lessons on Colour, &c., but while the child is always carefully exercised as indicated, in the lessons on Colour, Form, &c., it is thought by many to be an advanced exercise to produce notes when called for, or to name a note when produced. That should not be so. Ability to answer these tests lies at the very root of advancement in the reading of music.

10. Musical sounds, and the notes representing those sounds, are called by the same names, the first seven letters of the alphabet, in this order—C, D, E, F, G, A, B. But this is only in **instrumental** music.

In **vocal** music, for the production of a good sound, a good vowel is required, and in repeating C, D, E, F, G, A, B, you will notice that the vowel sound **ee** is the only one used throughout except in the case of F and A.

In **singing**, syllabic names are used which give a variety of good vowel sounds; the names are

Do, Re, Mi, Fa, So, La, Si. In reading these

    o is to be pronounced like **o** in **lone**.
    e   ,,   ,,   ,, **ay** in **ray**.
    i   ,,   ,,   ,, **ee** in **see**.
    a   ,,   ,,   ,, **a** in **father**.

So is sometimes written **Soh**, and sometimes **Sol**; **Si** is sometimes written **Ti**.

11. You require now to commit to memory both the alphabetic and the syllabic names, and also to note the syllabic name corresponding to each alphabetic name, and *vice versâ*. For this purpose they are written down together, and an eighth one is added in each case (the name being the same as the first), for reasons to come later on.

C	D	E	F	G	A	B	C
Do.	Re	Mi	Fa	So	La	(Si or Ti)	Do
1	2	3	4	5	6	7	8

Commit both sets of names to memory, both in the order from 1 to 8, and in reverse order from 8 to 1.

An extended use of the syllabic names is given later on. (See Art. 157a.)

12. Then as there are only these seven names, are there only seven notes, and can they represent only seven musical sounds? Not so: you saw in Arithmetic there are only the figures 1 to 9 to represent numbers, but yet we can represent millions of numbers by these nine figures by using the same figures again and again **in different positions.**

In a somewhat similar manner we can represent several musical sounds, by the seven notes whose names are given, by using them again and again in different positions, but in music the difference of position is not produced by moving from right to left, or the contrary, as in Arithmetic, but by moving up or down in a vertical direction to indicate higher and lower musical sounds respectively.

13. Taking the ordinary limits of the human voice, that is, from the lower notes ordinarily produced by a man's voice to the higher notes ordinarily produced by a woman's voice, it is found that the range is about 24 musical sounds. This does not include the very low or the very high musical sounds, produced by men and women of exceptional musical ability.

14. To represent these various sounds and their relation to one another with respect to one being higher or lower than another, a number of horizontal parallel lines are taken, so that by placing a note on each line and a note on each space between the lines, with one or two notes above the upper line, and one or two below the lower line, we are able to represent about 24 musical sounds at one view.

For this purpose eleven lines are taken, and you will notice that beginning with the lowest and ascending up to the highest is like going up the steps of a staircase.

These eleven lines and the spaces form what is called the **Great Staff**, a representation of which is given here, with the notes placed on it.

F G A B C D E F G A B C D E F G A B C D E F G

15. It would be difficult to tell at a glance, with certainty and with rapidity, which is the sixth, seventh, fourth, eighth, &c., line or space; so to make it easy to tell this, the middle line of the eleven is always omitted, except it is actually necessary to place a note on it, and then only a very short piece of the line is put in just where it is wanted, thus:—

F G A B C D E F G A B C D E F G A B C D E F G

16. This divides the **Great Staff** into two separate sections each containing five lines and four spaces; each of these sections is itself called a Staff. The upper five lines are called the **Upper Staff**; the lower five lines are called the **Lower Staff**.

The Upper Staff is also called the **Treble Staff**; the notes to be sung by the voices of women and children are placed on it.

The Lower Staff is called the **Bass Staff**; the notes to be sung by men's voices are placed on it.

17. If you name the notes beginning with the lower line of the Great Staff (Art. 14) and proceeding to the upper line, you will notice that every eighth note bears the same name. (See Art. 12.)

The eighth note from any given note is called the **Octave** of that note. The whole range of notes from any one note to the eighth above, or the eighth below it, is also called an **Octave**. The difference in sound between a note and the eighth above it or below it is also called an **Octave**.

18. Observe the short line shown between the Upper Staff and the Lower Staff (Art. 15). If the lines of the Great Staff be numbered consecutively from the lowest to the highest, this will be the sixth line; if they be numbered consecutively from the highest to the lowest it will also be the sixth line. In other words, there are five lines below it and five lines above it, so that it stands *in the middle*. Hence it is called the **middle line** of the Great Staff.

19. Referring to the Great Staff (Art. 14) we find C on it four times, and one of those times it is found on this middle line. This C so found is called **Middle** C.

20. If we wish to write a piece of Music containing only notes that can be sung by a Treble voice (Art. 6), since all these notes can be placed on the Treble Staff or upper section of the Great Staff, it would be useless, in fact it would only be waste of space, to write the lower section of the Great Staff, as there would be no notes to place on it, and consequently it is not written in such a case.

On the other hand, if we wish to write a piece of Music containing only notes that can be sung by men's voices, only the lower section of the Great Staff is used, the upper one being omitted.

21. Hence we frequently find sections of the Great Staff each consisting of five lines and four spaces, but when that is so, we require some mark to indicate whether it is the upper or lower section that is used.

Such a mark is called a **Clef**. The word clef means **a key**, and as you will see presently, the clef, when we know it, is the **key** to the names of the notes on the staff.

22. The clef used to denote that we are using the Upper Staff, or Treble Staff, is called the **Treble Clef**.

It is written thus:—

Though it crosses all the lines of the staff, it crosses the second line oftener than any other; so it is said to be placed on the second line. If you refer again to the Great Staff (Art. 14), you will see that this is its eighth line, and the note G is on it. Hence the Treble Clef is also called the **G Clef**. So that when we see this clef on any line, we know that G is the note on that line, and by naming the notes upwards and downwards from G, putting a note on each line and one on each space, we find the names of all the notes on the Treble Staff.

To do this expeditiously you should be quite familiar with Art. 11. Refer to it now and commit the names of the notes to memory thoroughly, both up and down, if you have not done so before.

23. The lines of a staff are distinguished from one another by their numbers; so are the spaces.

Both lines and spaces are numbered from the lowest to the highest; so that the first line is the lowest, and so on as you see them numbered below.

C D E F G A B C D E F G

24. The names of the notes on the five lines of the Treble Staff are
E G B D F
1 2 3 4 5

E G B D F

The names of the notes on the four spaces of Treble Staff are F A C E
                      1 2 3 4

If we want to write a note lower than E on the first line, place it immediately below the first line; this note would be D. See diagram in Art. 23.

The next note lower than this D is C; this is Middle C (See Art. 19), so we use a small piece of the middle line of the Great Staff to place C on it, as seen in the diagram in Art. 23, and in Art. 15.

A note may also be placed immediately above the fifth line; what note would that be? (See Art. 23.)

25. The clef used to denote the Lower Staff is written thus:— It is placed on the fourth line, and if you refer again to the Great Staff you will find that F is the note on this line.

Hence this is called the **F Clef,** and as it reminds us that F is the note on the fourth line, it gives us the key to the names of all the notes on both lines and spaces of this staff.

This is also called the **Bass Clef,** because it is used at the beginning of the staff on which the notes to be sung by the Bass voices of men are placed.

26. Writing the Lower or Bass Staff, with the F Clef, numbering the lines and spaces as directed in Art. 23, then naming the notes both upwards and downwards from F, and writing them down as named, till we have a note on each line, and on each space, thus:—

We see that the notes on the five lines of the Bass Staff are
    G B D F A.
    1 2 3 4 5.

The notes on the four spaces of the Bass Staff are   A C E G.
            1 2 3 4.

Here you should commit to memory thoroughly the names of the notes on the five lines of the Treble and Bass Staves respectively, also of the notes on the four spaces of the Treble and Bass Staves respectively, and exercise yourself well on them till you can tell with great rapidity the name of any note that may be pointed out to you.

27. Besides the highest kind of voices of women called **Treble** or **Soprano,** and the lowest voices of men called **Bass** voices, there are other qualities of voices.

28. There is the **Alto,** also a woman's voice, but not capable of reaching so high as the Soprano or Treble voice, though it can descend to lower notes than a Treble voice can.

There is also the **Tenor,** a man's voice, but not capable of reaching so low as the Bass voice, though it can ascend to higher notes than the Bass voice can.

29. We have seen in Arts. 20 to 26 that in order to be able to write on one staff of five lines and four spaces the notes that can be sung by either a Treble or a Bass voice, we take a section of the Great Staff, consisting of the upper five lines in the case of the Treble voices, and of the lower five lines in the case of the Bass voices.

30. In the case of voices not so high as the Treble or not so low as the Bass, and keeping the same object in view, viz., to write upon one staff of five lines and four spaces all the notes that can be sung by that one class of voice, we again take a section of the Great Staff, but this time neither the extreme upper nor the extreme lower five lines.

31. To suit Alto voices the three upper lines and the three lower lines of the Great Staff are not used, as shown by the dotted lines in the margin, but a staff of five lines is selected from the very middle of the Great Staff. These are shown by the black lines in the margin. Refer to the Great Staff, Art. 14, and you will observe that C, that is Middle C, is on the third of the lines selected above.

A clef called the **C Clef, Alto,** is placed on this line, and reminds us that C is the note on that line.

This clef is written thus:—   or

By naming and writing down the notes as in Arts. 23 and 26 we find the notes on the lines of this staff to be—
    F A C E G.
    1 2 3 4 5.

You must be careful not to pass this point till you make yourself quite familiar with the fact that the C shown here is the middle C, and is the same note as that shown **below the Staff** in the Diagram in Art. 23.

The notes on the four spaces of this staff are— G B D F.
           1 2 3 4.

Before leaving this staff observe that it is composed of the upper two lines of the Bass Staff: the F and A lines; the lower two of the Treble Staff, viz., the E and G lines, and between the first two and second two there is the middle line of the Great Staff, not usually written except in this staff, and in the one treated of in the next Article.

32. For Tenor voices a section of the Great Staff is chosen a little lower down as shown in the margin; it comprises the lower line of the Treble Staff, the Middle C line (written in this case) and the upper three lines of the Bass Staff.

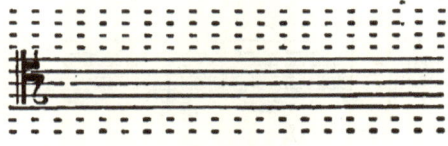

The clef is placed on the fourth or C line, and is in this case called the **C Clef, Tenor.** Though placed on a different line it is written in the same way as the C Clef, Alto. (See Art. 31.)

Though the lines of the Great Staff not used here or in previous Article are shown by dotted lines, it is to be clearly understood that in an actual piece of Music they would not appear at all. They are only shown here to indicate more clearly that each staff of five lines is a section from some part of the Great Staff of eleven lines, and also to show from what part of the Great Staff each of the smaller ones is taken.

By naming and writing down the names of the notes upward and downward from C we find the names of the notes on the five lines of the C Clef Tenor are—

D F A C E.
1 2 3 4 5.

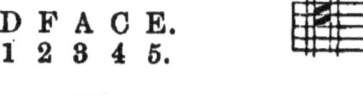

The names of the notes on the four spaces of the C Clef Tenor are— E G B D.
1 2 3 4.

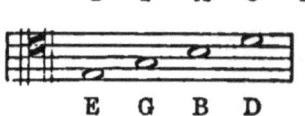

33. The Pitch of a musical sound means its **acuteness** or **gravity**; that is, whether it is high or low, and how high, or how low. Thus G on the second line of the Treble Clef is of higher pitch than E on the first line: while E in the fourth space of the same clef is of higher pitch than C in the third space; and F in the first space is of lower pitch than A in the second space, and so on.

For the sake of comparison, we have in the following a passage written at **the same pitch** in four different clefs. You should study this very carefully, noting particularly the position of Middle C in each clef.

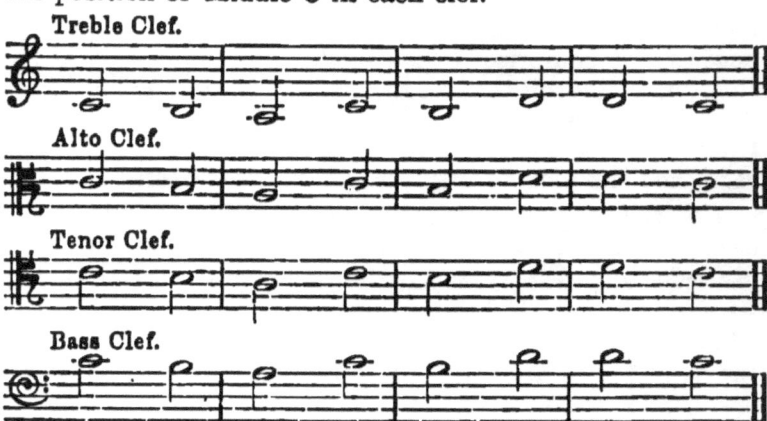

34. Very frequently the notes for Alto and Tenor voices are written on a staff with the Treble Clef. When this is so the writing for the Tenor is an octave higher than it should be, so there is usually a sign prefixed to indicate that the Tenor part is to be sung an octave lower than it is written, thus:—

Tenor 8ve. lower.

35. When the Music for each of the four voices is written on a separate staff the Music is said to be written in **Full Score**.

36. It is said to be in **Short Score** when, as frequently happens, the Soprano and Alto parts are written on one staff, the Treble; and when the Bass and Tenor parts are written on one staff, the Bass.

The following extract is first written in Short Score and then in Full Score.

Short Score:—

Full Score:—

Treble Clef.
Alto Clef.
Tenor Clef.
Bass Clef.

37. Sometimes a voice is capable of singing notes above or below the limits of the staff on which notes are usually written for it.

Many Soprano voices can go above G, the highest note written in Art. 28. To write notes higher, we use short pieces of lines above the staff, bearing in mind that as in the case of the lines of the staff, notes are to be placed not only on these short lines, but also in the spaces between them.

These little lines are called **Leger Lines**, from a French word **léger**, signifying **light**, because they present a **light** appearance, in contrast with the usual long **heavy** black lines of the staff.

By means of their use you see represented above, the notes A, B, C, higher than G, the highest note written in Art. 28.

Here I find it necessary to caution students against the erroneous notion that in writing the note C shown above, one leger line would be enough to show; by writing it in the position it now occupies it should be clearly seen that it is **above** the line on which A is placed, and this can only be done by writing the A line, as well as the C line, as you see done above.

If the leger line beneath the one on which the note C is placed above were not written, any examiner would read the note as A, and not as C, notwithstanding that it is placed so much higher up than the previous A; so be it understood that when only one leger line is written only one will be read. The same caution applies also to leger lines below the staff.

38. Observe carefully that the leger lines below the Treble Staff are:—First the Middle C line; then the upper or fifth line of the Bass Staff; then the fourth line of the Bass Staff, and so on.

On the other hand, leger lines above the Bass Staff are:—First the Middle C line, then the first or lower line of the Treble Staff; then the second line of the Treble Staff, and so on.

39. In the margin we have the note G, said to be written on the Bass Staff because it is on a leger line above, but in connection with, the Bass Staff.

Here we have the same note, and exactly the same pitch written on the Treble Staff; the third leger line above the Bass Staff being in reality a piece cut out of the G line of the Treble Staff.

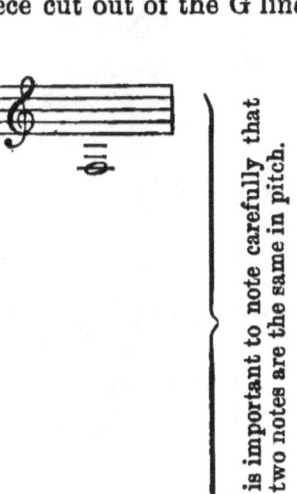

It is important to note carefully that these two notes are the same in pitch.

Again, what note is this? To answer, look at first leger line below the staff; this is Middle C line.

Next note below C? B. That is in the space.

Next note below B? A. That is on the second leger line.

Next note below A? G. That is in the space below second leger line.

Next note below G? F. That is the given note.

Express this note, same pitch on the Bass Staff. Here it is:—

It is important to note carefully that these two notes are the same in pitch.

Express the same note an octave higher on the Bass Staff.

Here it is easily done by naming the notes from F up to F; that is F, G, A, B, C, D, E, F, and allowing a line or a space for each, using as many leger lines as you find necessary. Whether is this new F on a line or a space? On a space.

Note carefully that this is the first space on Treble Staff. Refer to Art. 24 and see that F is the note for that space.

Write the following in the Bass Clef to sound two octaves lower.

This is a class of question frequently set at examinations.

In answering this type of question, be careful to note:—

1. Whether the passage is to be written in the Bass or Treble Clef.
2. Whether it is to be written higher, or lower, or at the same pitch.
3. The number of octaves it is to be written above or below its original pitch.

The following shows the notes as given, and then each written two octaves lower on the Bass Clef.

As given on Treble Staff.

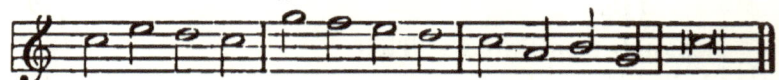

Two octaves lower on the Bass Staff.

Another example:—

Write the following at **the same pitch** on the Treble Staff.

Answer:—

Remember that the first leger line below the Treble Staff and the first leger line above the Bass Staff are the **same** line, and denote the **same pitch**.

40. In Art. 13 the ordinary range of the human voice was pointed out, but that is far from being the extreme range, in either the upward or downward direction. Some voices are capable of singing notes far above the highest given in Art. 14, and others are capable of singing notes far below the lowest there given.

From the lowest C shown on the second leger line below the Great Staff in the margin, to the highest C given on the second leger line above the Great Staff, that is four octaves, may be taken as the extreme limits of the human voice; all  the intervening C's are inserted in the diagram for the purpose of showing at a glance the number of octaves included between these extremes (see Art. 17 for meaning of octave) and also for the purpose of being able to speak about these various octaves. The C's from the lowest to the highest you will observe are numbered respectively 1, 2, 3, 4, 5. The notes within these various octaves are sometimes spoken of and written about when they are not placed on the staff.

When that is the case the notes of one octave are distinguished from those of another thus:—

The octave beginning with C_1 is called the Great Octave, and the notes are indicated by capital letters, as C, D, E, F, &c.

The octave beginning with C_2 is called the Small Octave, and the notes are indicated by small letters, as c, d, e, f, &c.

The octave beginning with C_3 is called the **one lined**, or **once marked** Octave; the notes in it are indicated by small letters with **one line** underneath, as c, d, e, f, &c.

The octave beginning with C_4 is called the **two lined**, or **twice marked** Octave; the notes in it are indicated by small letters with **two lines** underneath, as c, d, e, f, &c.

The octave beginning with C_5 is called the **three lined** Octave, and so on.

The lines here stated to be placed under the letters, are just as frequently placed over them with the same meaning as $\overline{\overline{c}}$, $\overline{\overline{d}}$, $\overline{\overline{e}}$, &c.

Another distinction made is this:—

The notes in the octave beginning with G_1 in the margin are said to be **In Alt.**

G_2 and notes above it are said to be **In Altissimo.**

Notes in the octave below C_1 in previous diagram are called the **Contra** or **Double Octave.**

Though the notes in this **Double Octave**, some of those **In Alt.** and those **In Altissimo,** cannot be produced by the human voice, they can, of course, be produced by musical instruments.

41. The whole range of notes over which any one voice can extend, from the lowest to the highest which it can produce, is called the **Compass** of that voice.

The following diagram shows the compass of each of the four principal kinds of

voice; though as before stated some exceptional Treble voices can go several notes higher than here indicated, but when that is so it nearly always happens that the quality of their lower notes is not so good. Similarly some exceptional Bass voices can go several notes below the limit here indicated, but when that is the case the quality of their upper notes is not usually so good. The case is somewhat similar with the Tenor and Alto voices.

Hints on answering the Questions on Chapter I.:—

    a. Aim at perfect legibility and neatness in writing all music exercises.

    b. The lines of the staff should be not more than one-eighth and not less than one-sixteenth of an inch apart.

c. When leger lines are used they should be the same distance apart as the lines forming the staff.

d. Do not omit necessary leger lines, as explained in Art. 37, but at the same time do not insert unnecessary ones. The D below the Treble Staff and the G above it do *not* need leger lines.

e. In answering questions like Nos. 24 to 30, first write down the names of the notes as they occur in the question, then close the book, and write the notes on a blank staff, afterwards correcting your writing by reference to the printed question.

f. Two adjacent notes of the scale, as G and A, or A and B are never written one immediately above the other. There is not enough space on the staff to show them clearly in that position. They are therefore written side by side. Remember this rule in answering Questions 11 and 12.

g. Notes which are an octave apart are *dissimilarly* placed on the staff, that is, one is on a line, the other in a space. Compare F (first *space* Treble Staff) and F above (fifth *line* Treble Staff) also F below (fourth *line* Bass Staff). Hence notes two octaves apart are *similarly* placed on the staff, that is they are either both on lines, or both in spaces. Notice this in connection with Questions 24–27.

CHAPTER II.

Time.—Accent.—Syncopation.

42. In the last chapter we saw that the **pitch** of a musical sound is indicated by the **position** on the staff occupied by the note representing the sound.

It is not sufficient to be able to represent the **pitch**; we also require to be able to indicate the **duration** of sound. This is done by using notes of different **shapes**, so that one fixed shape will indicate a very long sound, another fixed shape will represent a very short sound, and various other fixed shapes will represent sounds of intermediate lengths between the very long and the very short.

43. The **shapes** used to indicate **duration** of sounds and the names of these shapes are the following:—

| ‖𝒐‖ | 𝒐 | 𝅗𝅥 | ♩ | ♪ | ♫ | 𝅘𝅥𝅰 | 𝅘𝅥𝅱 |

Breve.   Semibreve.   Minim.   Crotchet.   Quaver.   Semi-quaver.   Demisemi-quaver.   Semidemi-semiquaver.

So that if you see a note G on the second line of a staff, or a note C on the third space, it may be represented by any one of the shapes above given, and the duration of the musical sound indicated will vary accordingly.

In writing the above notes the upright line is called a stem, and the line making an angle with it is called a hook. The stem may be turned either upward or downward as

𝅘𝅥   𝅘𝅥

When the music for only one "part" or "voice" is written on a staff as in the Full Score extract on page 11 the rule is:—All notes below the middle line have upward stems; all notes above it have downward stems; while notes on that line have sometimes upward and sometimes downward stems.

But when the music for two parts or voices is written on one staff, as in the Short Score extract on page 11, the rule is:—All notes belonging to the upper part have upward stems, while those of the lower part have downward stems. It sometimes happens that the same note is common to both parts, then it will have both an upward and a downward stem, thus:—

In writing these notes, hold the pen in the opposite direction to that usually adopted in ordinary writing, viz., with the point of the nib inclining towards the left hand. A broad-nibbed pen is best. Form the head of the note first, and make the stems, *not slanting* but *upright*, and just *touching* the heads, not *drawn through* them, or placed so that if produced they would *pass through* the heads.

In *printed* music, when the stems are turned *upwards* they are placed on the *right* of the heads as ♩♩ not ♩♩; when downwards, on the left of the heads as ♩♩ not ♩♩.

The hooks of quavers, &c., must always be placed on the *right-hand* side of the stem, whether turned upwards or downwards, as:—

But in *manuscript* music the most convenient method—and a very generally adopted one—is to place the stems *always* on the right side of the note, whether the stem is upward or downward. This rule is a very easy one to remember, and the notes, when written in this way may be made to have quite as neat an appearance as when the printers' rule is followed.

There are exceptions to this general rule as to the placing of both stems and hooks, when notes are grouped and written together so that the hook of one note meets that of the next to it.

44. The Breve or Double note, ‖𝆏‖, is the longest note, and is only used in Church Music.

The Semibreve, or Whole note, 𝅝, is the longest note in general use, and two semibreves are equal in length to one breve.

The Minim, or Half note, 𝅗𝅥, is half the length of the semibreve.

The Crotchet, or Quarter note, ♩, is half the length of the minim.

The Quaver, or Eighth note, ♪, is half the length of the crotchet.

The Semiquaver, or Sixteenth note, 𝅘𝅥𝅯, is half the length of the quaver.

The Demisemiquaver, or Thirty-second note, 𝅘𝅥𝅰, is half the length of the semiquaver.

The Semidemisemiquaver, or Sixty-fourth note, 𝅘𝅥𝅱, is half the length of the demisemiquaver.

Putting the same thing another way:

A Semibreve is equal to two minims, or four crotchets, or eight quavers, &c.

A Minim is equal to two crotchets, or four quavers, or eight semiquavers, &c.

A Crotchet is equal to two quavers, or four semiquavers, or eight demisemiquavers, and so on.

The relative lengths of these various notes may be conveniently expressed as in the following table:—

	Semibreves.	Minims.	Crotchets.	Quavers.	Semiquavers.	Demisemiquavers.	Semidemisemiquavers.
𝄎 =	2	4	8	16	32	64	128
𝅝 =		2	4	8	16	32	64
𝅗𝅥 =			2	4	8	16	32
♩ =				2	4	8	16
♪ =					2	4	8
𝅘𝅥𝅯 =						2	4
𝅘𝅥𝅰 =							2

45. It will be seen from the above that each note from the longest to the shortest is **twice the length** of the next shorter note; and each note from the shortest to the longest is **half the length** of the next longer note.

From this it would appear, that if we desire to indicate that any particular sound should be longer or shorter than it is, we have no way of doing so unless we make it **twice as long**, or **half as long**, and that would be so if there were no means of indicating duration of sound, except as just explained, but there are additional ways. (See Arts. 46, 47, and 164.)

46. If a dot be placed after a note it makes the note half as long again, as 𝅗𝅥. is now a minim and a half, or three crotchets. A note with a dot after it, like that, is called a **dotted note**; the one just used is a **dotted minim**. A **dotted crotchet** ♩. is equal to a crotchet and a-half, that is, to three quavers.

If a **second dot** be added, it adds to the original note quarter its length, that is half as much as the first dot. A third dot is hardly ever used, but if used it adds to the original note **one-eighth** of its length, that is half as much as the second dot.

A **double dotted minim** 𝅗𝅥.. is equal to a minim and a-half and a-quarter; that is equal to two crotchets and one crotchet and a quaver; or equal to **three crotchets and a quaver**.

Observe that the dots herein referred to are placed **after** the note, that is to the **right-hand side** of it; if placed **above** the note or **below** it, the dots have quite a different meaning. (See vocabulary, **Staccato**.)

47. Another method of lengthening a sound to any desired extent is by means of the **Tie**.

A **Tie** is a curved line, placed over or under two notes **of the same pitch**, as in the margin, to indicate that the first one is  to be **prolonged** by the length of the second one, which is not sung or played as a separate note at all.

In such a case the second note may be the same length as the first, or longer, or shorter, and the **Tie** may be repeated any number of times, thus prolonging the length of any one sound to any extent desired. Notes thus connected are said to be **tied.**

Observe that the **Tie** (or **Bind** as it is sometimes called) is only used to connect notes **of the same pitch.**

A curved line is often used to connect notes of **different pitch,** but then it has a different meaning altogether. (See vocabulary, **Slur.**)

48. By referring to Art. 1 you will see that we require characters to indicate **Silence,** as well as notes to indicate Sounds, and there are such characters used.

The characters used to indicate silence are called **Rests.**

Each note used to indicate **Duration of Sound** has a corresponding **Rest** to indicate **Duration of Silence** for the same length of time. The following shows the rest corresponding to each note :—

It is very important to learn the position on the staff in which the rests are usually placed, so you should give it careful attention at once. On the Bass, or other staff, they would be placed on lines or spaces of the same number as shown here on the Treble Staff.

Some have a difficulty in remembering the difference in shape between a crotchet rest and a quaver rest; the crochet rest having the hook to the right at the top of the stem, and the quaver rest having the hook turned towards the left at the top of the stem.

If you will bear in mind that *q* is the initial of *quaver*, and that the quaver rest is somewhat like a badly-formed *q* in writing, and therefore has the hook towards the left, you cannot forget the difference between them.

Rests are lengthened by the use of one or more dots placed after them, in exactly the same way as notes; when so lengthened they are called **Dotted Rests**.

49. Pieces of Music are said to be of **equal time length** when the time values of the notes contained in them are the same.

By a reference to Art. 44 you will see the equivalents of each note, so that, taking for instance a semibreve, we say

$$\circ = \text{𝅗𝅥 𝅗𝅥, or 𝅗𝅥 ♩ ♩, or 𝅗𝅥 ♩ ♪ ♪, or ♩ ♩ ♩ ♪ ♪}$$

Hence we say that five pieces of Music are equal in time length if each contains a semibreve or its equivalent in any of the forms just set down, or in several other forms in which the equivalent of a semibreve might be set down.

60. Every musical composition, no matter how long, is divided into small parts of equal length called **Measures**, by vertical lines drawn across the staff, thus:—

These vertical lines are called **Bars**.

The spaces between them are called **Measures**, and, as before stated, the measures are of **equal time length**.

The vertical lines are often called **Bar Lines**, and the spaces between them are called **Bars**. Perhaps the name bars is applied oftener than measures to these equal divisions, but by whichever name they are called they must all be of equal length, except perhaps the **first** and the **last**, which individually may or may not be equal to the others.

But if the first be unequal, the last must be unequal also, and then the first and last together must be equal to one of the other bars or measures.

61. The length of a bar or measure is frequently equal to the semibreve or whole note. When the length of each bar in a piece of Music is not that of a semibreve, it has always a relation to the length of the semibreve.

For the purpose of expressing this relation accurately, it is usual to give a numerical value to each note. A semibreve is usually assigned **four** as its value.

The semibreve, then, will be sung or played while one counts **four**; thus, **one, two, three, four.**

If one be singing he cannot very well count at the same time. In that case he measures time by motions of the hand produced in the same time as one counts; these motions are called **Beats**.

The direction of the motions of the hand in beating time, are shown in the diagram in the margin, viz., down, left, right, up; down, left, right, up, and so on continuously through the whole piece.

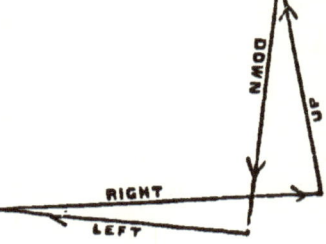

A semibreve, then, is to be understood as being ordinarily equal to four beats, or counts.

52. A reference to Art. 44 will now enable you to tell how many beats or counts go to a minim. How many? Two?

How many to a crotchet? One.

How many to a quaver? Half a beat.

How many semiquavers to one beat? Four.

53. If this plan were strictly and invariably followed, you can see that in some instances it might be necessary to sing or play not only four notes, but even eight, or sixteen to one beat, and if you ever try to do this you will readily admit that it is difficult.

54. To obviate this difficulty, in pieces of Music in which the quaver and notes shorter than the quaver are in the majority, it is usual to arrange that a shorter note than the crotchet may be the equivalent of one beat or one count, and this reduces the number of notes that go to one beat. After what has been said in Art. 52 this may seem strange, but observe that in beating time, **down, left, right, up,** or in counting time, **one, two, three, four,** we may do so either quickly or slowly; either very quickly or very slowly, so that a beat or a count may be very different at one time from what it is at another, and though the beats or counts may not vary in length throughout the whole of the same passage, they may vary very much in different passages.

So far nothing has been said as to the *actual* length of a beat or of a bar, that is, the part of a second of time, or the number of seconds of time occupied by the one or the other; this is reserved for Art. 78, which see, and after that has been studied the above plan will not appear strange or improper, because what has been said so far has reference only to *relative* lengths of notes.

55. When a semibreve is the equivalent of a bar as stated in Art. 51 there are four beats to the bar; when a semibreve is not the equivalent of a bar, then the bar is considered as being equal to some fraction of the semibreve,

and the fraction may be either proper or improper. Thus a bar may be ¾ of a semibreve. Now what does ¾ (**three-fourths**) of a semibreve mean? By drawing on your knowledge of fractions you will recollect that 4, the denominator, shows into how many equal parts the unit (which in this case is the semibreve) has been divided; so that here it is divided into four equal parts. What is the fourth part of a semibreve? A crotchet (see Art. 44).

Then the numerator 3 shows how many of these equal parts are taken to form the fraction. So that in this case the ¾ means three crotchets are the equivalent of a bar. In such a case there would be three beats or counts in a bar, each being value for one crotchet.

How would you count the time of such music?

One, two, three; one, two, three; &c.

How would you beat the time of it? **Down, left, up; down, left, up,** &c. Or it might be **down, right, up; down, right, up,** &c.

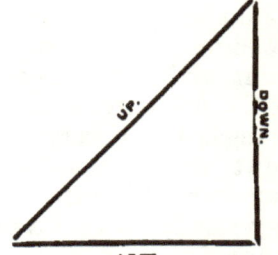

Again, a bar may be 3/2 of a semibreve; what does this mean? The 2 means that the semibreve is divided into two equal parts, and the 3 shows there are three of such parts in the bar.

When a semibreve is divided into two equal parts each part is a minim (see Art. 44), so that in this case there would be three minims in a bar.

How would you beat the time then? Same as in ¾ time, **down, left, up; down, left, up,** &c., but the beats would be slower.

Or again, the bar may be 2/4 of a semibreve; what does this mean? The 4 shows that the semibreve is divided into four equal parts; each part is a crotchet (see Art. 44); the 2 then shows that there are two crotchets in a bar.

How would you beat the time then? **Down, up; down, up,** &c.

How would you count it? **One, two; one, two,** &c.

If you have accustomed yourself to calling the notes by the second names given in Art. 44, viz., **whole note** for semibreve, **half note** for minim, &c., you will recognise at once the meaning of these fractional numbers used to represent time. Thus $\frac{3}{4}$ = **three quarter notes** in a bar, $\frac{4}{2}$ = **four half notes** in a bar, and so on.

56. Each beat in a bar is usually value for either a minim, or a crotchet, or a quaver; or a dotted minim, or a dotted crotchet, or a dotted quaver.

57. The number of beats to the bar, with the **value** of each beat, constitute what is called the **Time** of any musical composition.

58. By **Value of a Beat** is meant the note, or dotted note, equal, in duration of time, to the beat.

By **Value of a Bar,** or **Measure,** is meant the number of notes, or dotted notes of a certain kind, in the bar.

59. A mark is placed at the beginning of each piece of Music as a guide to indicate the time of the piece. This mark is called the **Time Signature.**

60. The Time Signature is usually a fraction, proper or improper (see Art. 55). There are two exceptions to this, one very common; the other not so common. (See Arts. 61-62.)

61. When there are **four** beats to the bar, **each** beat being value for a **minim,** or half-note, so that the value of a bar is four minims, or four half-notes, the signature is $\frac{4}{2}$, as in the following example:—

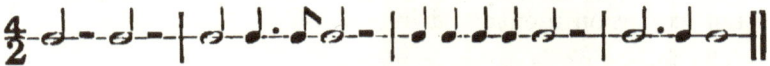

When there are **four** beats to the bar, **each** beat being value for a **crotchet,** or quarter-note, so that the whole bar is value for four crotchets, or four quarter-notes (= one semibreve or whole note), the signature is $\frac{4}{4}$, but is often **C,** as it is called **Common Time.** This is one of the exceptions mentioned in Art. 60.

The following is an example of ¼ time, using only one line of the staff for the sake of convenience:—

The following is another example of the same, using **C** as signature:—

The numerical time-signature is preferable to the **C**, as being much more definite in its signification.

Observe carefully that though the value of each bar is four crotchets, it is not necessary that four crotchets and nothing else should be written. The **equal** of crotchets may be written in almost any form, with slight limitations, which can only be understood after you have learned Accent.

A similar observation applies to all the following examples, and to all those which you may write yourself in answering the Questions.

When there are **four** beats to the bar, **each** beat being value for a **quaver**, or eighth-note, so that the value of a bar is four quavers, or four eighth-notes, the signature is ⅜, as in the following example:—

62. When there are **two** beats to the bar, **each** beat being value for a **minim**, or half-note, so that the value of the bar is two minims, or two half-notes, ⅔ is the signature, but it may be, and often is, . This is the other exception mentioned in Art. 60.

The following is an example:—

When ₵ is the signature the time is called **Alla Breve Time**, and sometimes **Tempo a Cappella**, because it is chiefly used in Church Music.

When there are **two** beats to the bar, **each** beat being value for a **crotchet**, or quarter-note, so that the value of the bar is two crotchets, or two quarter-notes, ⅔ is the signature (see Art. 55).

The following is an example :—

[musical example in 2/4]

When there are **two** beats to the bar, **each** beat being value for a **quaver**, or eighth-note, so that the value of a bar is two quavers, or two eighth-notes, ⅔ is the signature. For explanation of fraction see Art. 55.

The following is an example :—

[musical example in 2/8]

63. When there are **two** beats to the bar, whatever may be the value of a beat, the time is called **Duple**.

When there are **four** beats to the bar, whatever may be the value of each beat, the time is called **Quadruple**.

When there are **three** beats to the bar, whatever may be the value of each beat, the time is called **Triple**.

64. When there are **three** beats to the bar, **each** beat being value for a **minim**, or half-note, so that the whole bar is value for three minims, or three half-notes, 3/2 is the signature.

The following is an example :—

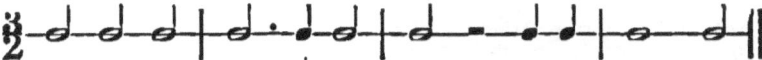

When there are **three** beats to the bar, **each** beat being value for a **crotchet**, or quarter-note, so that the whole bar is of the value of three crotchets, or three quarter-notes, ¾ is the signature.

The following is an example :—

[musical example in 3/4]

When there are **three** beats to the bar, **each** beat being value for a **quaver,** or eighth-note, so that the whole bar is of the value of three quavers, or three eighth-notes, ¾ is the signature. (See Art. 55 for a full explanation of fraction.)

The following is an example :—

[musical notation example in 3/8 time]

Observe carefully if the value of the bar be three crotchets, the bar may consist either of three crotchets or their equivalents, in almost any form, with slight limitations, which can only be understood after you have learned about Accent. The case is similar when the value of the bar is three minims or three quavers.

65. The three kinds of time already explained, with their sub-divisions, are all called **Simple Time.**

So that there may be **Simple Duple Time,**
Simple Quadruple Time,
Simple Triple Time.

Let us see the meaning of the word **Simple.**

You will have noticed that in the kinds of time mentioned in Arts. 61 to 64, the value of a beat is in each case a minim, or a **crotchet,** or a quaver. You also know that

2 minims make a semibreve, or 1 minim $= \frac{1}{2}$ a semibreve,
4 crotchets ,, ,, or 1 crotchet $= \frac{1}{4}$ a semibreve,
8 quavers ,, ,, or 1 quaver $= \frac{1}{8}$ a semibreve,

that is, some integral number of either minims, or crotchets, or quavers, makes a semibreve.

Using arithmetical language, then, we say that each of these notes is an **Aliquot Part** of a semibreve, and consequently the value of a beat in each of the kinds of time already enumerated is an aliquot part of a semibreve. That is what is meant by the term **Simple.**

66. Referring to Art. 56 we find that the value of a beat may be a **dotted** minim, or a **dotted** crotchet, or a **dotted** quaver.

Is there any integral number (any **whole** number) of dotted minims, or of dotted crotchets, or of dotted quavers that equal a semibreve? No. (Work this out arithmetically yourself.)

Then when the beat is value for a dotted minim, or a dotted crotchet, or a dotted quaver, it is not an aliquot part of a semibreve. The time is then called **Compound**. Compare with Art. 65, and see difference between Simple and Compound Time. In Simple Time each beat is value for a **simple note**, an aliquot part of a semibreve, but in Compound Time each beat is value for a **dotted note**, which is not an aliquot part of a semibreve.

67. As Simple Time may be Duple, or Triple, or Quadruple, so **Compound Time** may be Duple, or Triple, or Quadruple: the following are examples:—

When there are **two** beats to the bar, **each** beat being value for a **dotted minim**, (= three crotchets = three quarter-notes), so that the whole bar is value for two dotted minims, (= six crotchets = six quarter-notes), then $\frac{6}{4}$ is the Time Signature.

The following is an example:—

When there are **two** beats to the bar, **each** beat being value for a **dotted crotchet** (= three quavers = three eighth-notes), so that the whole bar is value for two **dotted crotchets**, (= six quavers = six eighth-notes), then $\frac{6}{8}$ is the Time Signature.

The following is an example:—

When there are **two** beats to the bar, **each** beat being value for a **dotted quaver** (= three semiquavers), so that the whole bar is value for two dotted quavers (= six semiquavers), then $\frac{6}{16}$ is the Time Signature.

The following is an example:—

The three foregoing are examples of **Compound Duple** Time.

68. When there are **four** beats to the bar, **each** beat being value for a **dotted minim** (= three crotchets = three quarter-notes), so that the whole bar is value for four dotted minims (= twelve crotchets = twelve quarter-notes), then $\frac{12}{4}$ is the Time Signature.

The following is an example:—

[musical notation in $\frac{12}{4}$ time]

When there are **four** beats to the bar, **each** beat being value for a **dotted crotchet** (= three quavers = three eighth-notes), so that the whole bar is value for four dotted crotchets (= twelve quavers = twelve eighth-notes), then $\frac{12}{8}$ is the Time Signature.

The following is an example:—

[musical notation in $\frac{12}{8}$ time]

When there are **four** beats to the bar, **each** beat being value for a **dotted quaver** (= three semiquavers = three sixteenth-notes), so that the whole bar is value for four dotted quavers (= twelve semiquavers = twelve sixteenth-notes), then $\frac{12}{16}$ is the Time Signature.

The following is an example:—

[musical notation in $\frac{12}{16}$ time]

The three foregoing are examples of **Compound Quadruple** Time.

69. When there are **three** beats to the bar, **each** beat being value for a **dotted minim** (= three crotchets = three quarter-notes), so that the whole bar is value for three dotted minims (= nine crotchets = nine quarter-notes), then $\frac{9}{4}$ is the Time Signature.

The following is an example:—

When there are **three** beats to the bar, **each** beat being value for a **dotted crotchet**, (= three quavers = three eighth-notes,) so that the whole bar is value for three dotted crotchets, (= nine quavers = nine eighth-notes,) then 9/8 is the Time Signature.

The following is an example:—

When there are **three** beats to the bar, **each** beat being value for a **dotted quaver**, (= three semiquavers = three sixteenth-notes,) so that the whole bar is value for three dotted quavers, (= nine semiquavers = nine sixteenth-notes,) then $\frac{9}{16}$ is the Time Signature.

The following is an example:—

The three foregoing are examples of **Compound Triple Time**.

The diligent student will not merely learn these things by heart, but will as he goes along examine each fraction given as a Time Signature, find what is the value of that fraction of a semibreve, and see that it corresponds with what is stated as the value of a bar. **(See Art. 55.)**

70. By some the name **Common Time** is applied only to Quadruple Time; by others it is applied to both Quadruple and Duple Time.

71. In beating Triple Time, as already explained, the beats are **down, left, up; down, left, up,** &c.; or it might be **down, right, up; down, right, up,** &c. In Quadruple Time the beats are **down, left, right, up; down, left, right, up,** &c. In Duple Time the beats are **down, up; down, up,** &c. There are some exceptions to this in **Compound** Time. For example, when the time is 6/8, so that there are six quavers to the bar, there are **sometimes**

D

six beats to the bar, each value for a quaver, instead of two beats, each value for a dotted crotchet, thus: **down, left, left, right, right, up; down, left, left, right, right, up**, &c.

Whether there are to be two beats or six beats depends upon the nature of Accent (see Arts. 76 and 77), and upon the rate of movement of the tune, but a full explanation of the matter belongs to the domain of practical music, so it will not be further discussed here.

72. Some will now be disposed to ask why there is a separate $\frac{6}{8}$ time signature, since $\frac{6}{8} = \frac{3}{4}$ and there should be no necessity for both? The reason of this will be clear after studying the Arts. on Accent. (See Arts. 73 to 77.) The same thing applies to $\frac{6}{4}$ and $\frac{3}{2}$ times, or to $\frac{6}{16}$ and $\frac{3}{8}$.

The following is a tabulated list of time signatures :—

SIMPLE.

Duple Time (two beats to the bar) $\frac{2}{2}$ or ₵, $\frac{2}{4}$, $\frac{2}{8}$.
Triple Time (three beats to the bar) $\frac{3}{2}$, $\frac{3}{4}$, $\frac{3}{8}$.
Quadruple Time (four beats to the bar) $\frac{4}{2}$, ₵ or $\frac{4}{4}$, $\frac{4}{8}$.

COMPOUND.

Duple Time (two beats to the bar) $\frac{6}{4}$, $\frac{6}{8}$, $\frac{6}{16}$.
Triple Time (three beats to the bar) $\frac{9}{4}$, $\frac{9}{8}$, $\frac{9}{16}$.
Quadruple Time (four beats to the bar) $\frac{12}{4}$, $\frac{12}{8}$, $\frac{12}{16}$.

73. As in reading, certain words and certain syllables in words, require a greater stress of the voice than others, and as in reading poetry this greater stress occurs with greater regularity, falling as a rule in some poetry on every second, and in other poetry on every third syllable, no matter how long the piece of poetry may be; so in Music, certain notes have a greater stress given to them than to others. This greater stress or force is called **Accent**, and the regular recurrence of the Accent in Music is called **Rhythm**.

As an example of the regular recurrence of this accent in poetry it may be sufficient to consider the following well-known lines of Gray :—

> The **cur-few tolls** the **knell** of **part**-ing **day**,
> The **low**-ing **herd** winds **slow**-ly **o'er** the **lea**.

Here the accent falls on every second syllable, and is indicated by the thick letters. It will be a useful exercise for the student to go carefully through the whole of Gray's Elegy, and he will be surprised at the regularity with which this accent recurs throughout the piece.

As an example of the recurrence of this accent on every third syllable the following may be taken from the Irish poet Moore:—

> As a **beam** o'er the **face** of the **wat**-ers may **glow**,
> While the **tide** runs in **dark**-ness and **cold**-ness be-**low**;
> So the **cheek** may be **ting'd** with a **warm** sunny **smile**,
> Though the **cold** heart to **ru**-in runs **dark**-ly the **while**.

Here again the accented syllables are indicated by thick letters.

74. No matter what species of time may be used, the first beat in each bar is accented, so that if we represent the accented parts of a bar by ∧ the accents would appear as follows in duple, triple, and quadruple times respectively:

Duple.

Triple.

Quadruple.

75. In ⁴⁄₄ (or C) time, the third beat in each bar also gets an accent though one not so important as the first; the accent on the first beat is then called the **Principal Accent**, and that on the third beat is called the **Secondary Accent**. So that if we represent the Secondary Accent by ! then the accents in ⁴⁄₄ time would be as follows:—

76. In Simple Duple or Triple time there is not usually any Secondary Accent in a bar; but in any species of time when there are several small notes repeatedly grouped together to form a beat,

the first note of each such group receives a very slight accent, less than the Secondary explained in Art. 75, and which might be called a **Sub-Secondary Accent**, though the term is new.

When **grouping** takes place, it is important to note that the number of groups in a bar should, as a rule, correspond with the number of beats in the bar, each group being of the value of a single beat, as in the following examples (*a*), (*b*), which are good, the corresponding examples (*c*), (*d*), being bad.

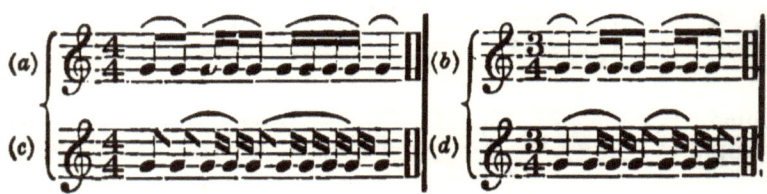

77. What species of time is ⅜ time? It is a Compound Duple Time. Being Duple, then, there are two beats to the bar, and as stated in Art. 76 only one accent to the bar, except as explained below.

What is the value of a bar of ⅜ time? Two **dotted crotchets** (= 6 quavers). Example:—

If written thus the beating of the time is simply **down, up; down, up,** &c., with the accent on the down beat; but it may be, and sometimes is, written in quavers, as

and then there may be six quick beats to the bar, viz., **down, left, left, right, right, up,** &c., with a Principal accent on the first beat and a Secondary accent on the fourth beat.

Hence in 6/8 time there may be either one or two accents in the bar, whereas in 3/4 time, being a triple time, there can be only one accented beat in the bar; there is a similar difference between 6/16 and 3/8 time. (See Art. 72.)

Whichever method of beating 6/8 time be adopted, if there be grouping of the notes, it is important to observe that it must be such as to admit of a division of the bar into two equal parts.

In Music you are not to expect to see any marks such as are used in Arts. 74, 75 and 77, to indicate the accented parts of the bar; no such marks are used, as you are expected to know accented parts sufficiently well without them.

Before leaving the subject of accent it should be explained that some musicians speak of accent in a way different from that given above. They say the kinds of accent are **strong, medium, and weak.** They give the name **strong** to what has just been called the Principal Accent, the name **medium** to what has been called the Secondary Accent, and they assign the **weak accent** to those parts of the bar which in the above have been considered as entirely unaccented.

Using these terms to indicate the different kinds of accents, the following table shows the order in which they occur in duple, triple and quadruple time respectively:—

Duple Time	Strong, weak.
Triple Time	Strong, weak, weak.
Quadruple Time ...	Strong, weak, medium, weak.

In the following examples, the positions of the strong, weak, and medium accents are marked by the letters s, w, and m, respectively.

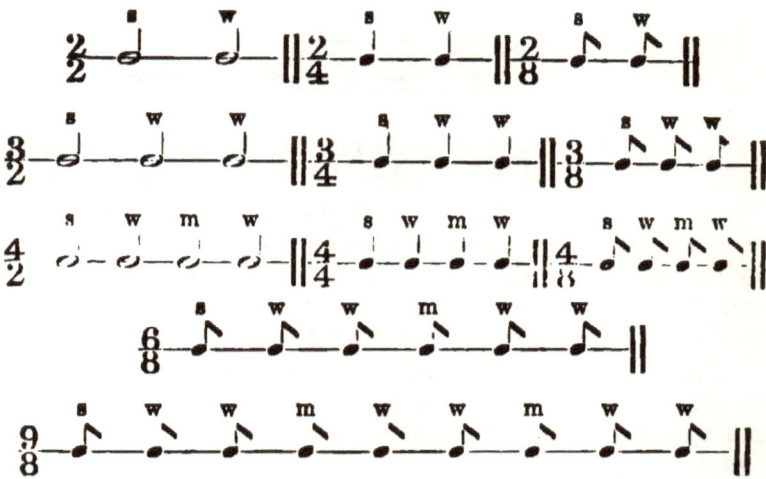

78. As stated in Art. 54, when we beat time we may do so quickly or slowly, so that to say that a piece of Music is in ¾ time, or any other kind of time, gives us no accurate information as to the quickness or slowness, that is, as to the **pace** with which the piece is to be sung or played.

To understand how this **pace** is actually determined and indicated it is necessary to understand first what a **Metronome** is.

A **Metronome** is, in its simplest form, a pendulum beating time by its oscillations; the longer any pendulum is, the slower it oscillates; the shorter the pendulum is, the quicker it oscillates; observe the clock: if it be going slow and you want to correct it by making the pendulum go more quickly, you turn a little screw on the lower end of the rod of the pendulum, which moves upward the ball (or bob as it is called) of the pendulum, and thus **shortens** it, then it oscillates faster and gains time. If the clock be already going fast you would turn the screw in the opposite direction letting the ball of the pendulum down lower, thus **lengthening** the pendulum: then it oscillates more slowly and the clock loses time.

If you require a homely, practical, but yet striking proof of this, take a piece of string 8 feet long, and tie a weight of, say, 1 oz. to one end of it, hold the other end coiled once or twice round your forefinger and holding up your hand, let the suspended weight oscillate freely to and fro; that is in reality a pendulum; count the oscillations, you can do it easily.

Now shorten the pendulum by catching the string within, say, 6 inches of the weight, hold your hand and let the shortened pendulum vibrate freely as before; you will now notice that it oscillates much more quickly, in fact you will have a difficulty in counting the oscillations. After this you will need no further proof that the longer a pendulum is, the more slowly it oscillates; the shorter a pendulum is, the more quickly it oscillates.

In applying this to the Metronome, or, indeed, to the clock, it is necessary to bear in mind that the pendulum consists of two parts, a long, slender **light** rod, and a comparatively **heavy** ball which is movable on the rod. The length of the pendulum is not the length of the rod, which remains the same, but the length from the point where the rod is suspended, to a point within the heavy ball. That is the reason why the pendulum is shortened or lengthened by moving the ball up or down on the rod. But though you can **observe** these things now, for a **full understanding** of them you must wait till you have made some progress in the study of Natural Philosophy.

On page 40 you have a representation of a Metronome; C D is the rod of the pendulum, a very thin narrow strip of steel, which as you see, is supported at its lowest point C, differing in this respect from other pendulums, which are suspended from their highest points, and which, therefore, when set in motion, oscillate under the influence of gravity, while the pendulum of the Metronome is made to oscillate by means of a spring, concealed within the instrument, but this in no way alters the law already laid down as to oscillation.

The part C E of the rod is hidden from our view by the wooden case of the instrument, and hence is represented by dotted lines; B is the ball of the pendulum, which can be moved up or down so as to lengthen or shorten the pendulum, the length, as already explained, being reckoned from C to B, not from C to D.

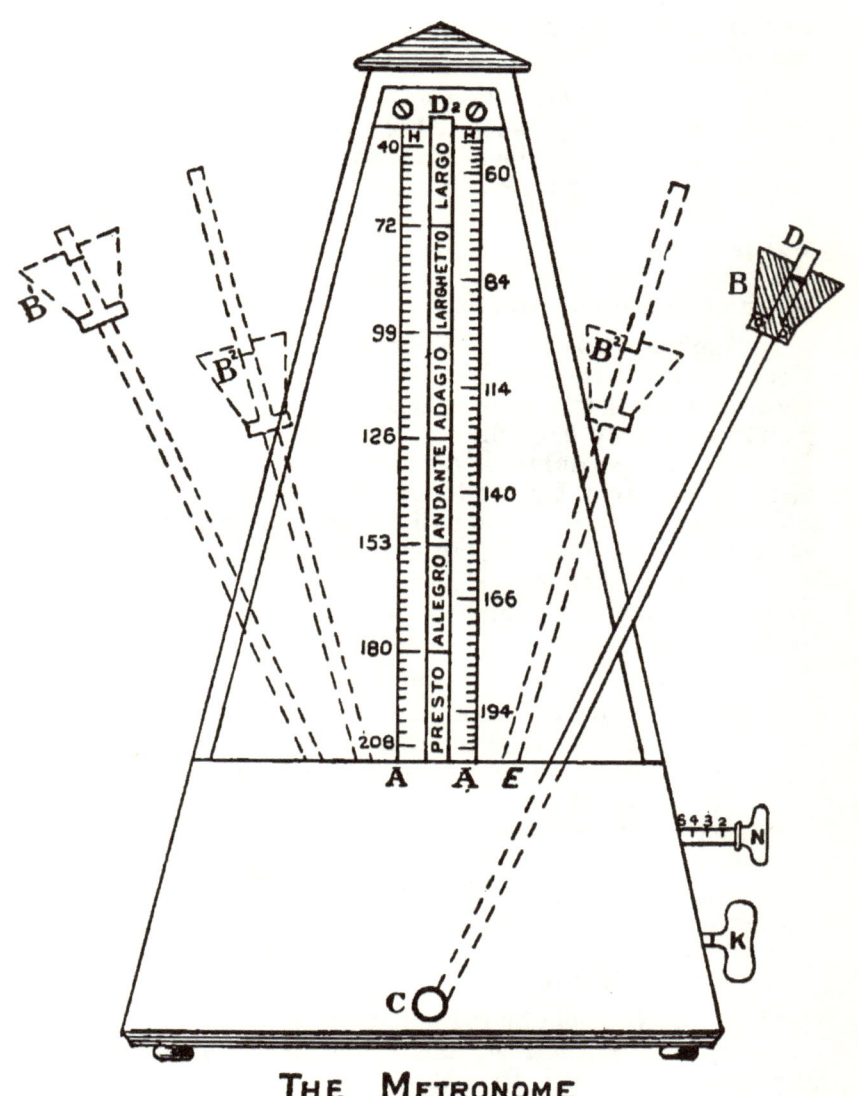

THE METRONOME

When the ball is in the position indicated by B, the pendulum is long, takes a wide range of swing, and oscillates from B on the right to the position shown as B^1 in dotted lines on the left; in such a position it oscillates slowly.

If the ball be moved down to the position indicated by B^2, the pendulum is shortened: the length is now from C to B^2: the pendulum does not now take such a wide range of swing, but oscillates from B^2 on the right to B^2 on the left, both shown in dotted lines: it then oscillates more quickly.

If the ball be moved lower down still, the pendulum will oscillate quicker still, and so on.

When at rest the pendulum stands in the vertical line $C D^2$.

A H is a plate of brass, or steel, polished and carefully graduated; the numbers placed on the right side and on the left are not two different sets of numbers, but one set, and they are so placed in order to prevent overcrowding and indistinctness.

What do these numbers signify? That is best answered by taking one as an example; take 72, let the rod of the pendulum stand in the vertical line $C D^2$, and move down the ball B till the black line across the rod near the upper end of the ball stands at 72; now set it in motion and the number of oscillations **per minute** will be 72. In like manner move the ball down to 114 and set the pendulum in motion; the number of oscillations **per minute** will now be 114.

Or, move the ball up to 40: the number of oscillations **per minute** is now 40; so that the figures indicate the number of oscillations **per minute** which the pendulum will make when the ball is fixed at the same height on the rod as the figures on the scale.

79. Now, if a composer wants to indicate that he wishes his composition to be sung or played at the rate of 90 crotchets per minute, he places at the beginning of the composition, over the Treble Staff, ♩ = 90: this is to indicate that the Metronome is to be set at 90, so that it will then beat 90 per minute, each beat is to be value for a **crotchet**, so that the duration of a crotchet is $\frac{1}{90}$ of a minute, or 90 crotchets are to be played or sung in a minute of time.

The same is expressed otherwise, thus:—

♩ = M 90 ; or M = 90 ♩ ; or M ♩ = 90.

If we meet ♪ = 120 M, or M ♪ = 120, or M = ♪ 120, what does it mean?

It means that the ball of the pendulum of the Metronome is to be adjusted to 120, the pendulum will then beat 120 per minute, and a **quaver** is to be the length of each beat of the pendulum: a quaver is thus the $\frac{1}{120}$ part of a minute, or in other words, 120 quavers are to be played or sung in a minute of time.

If the time be compound we might meet such a sign as the following: ♩. = M 70. From what has just been said you will understand this means that 70 dotted crotchets are to be played or sung in a minute of time.

80. Completing the description of the Metronome, K is a key which winds up the clockwork inside the frame, N is a knob marked with the figures 2, 3, 4, 6, and which can be pushed in or pulled out at pleasure; if pushed in to 4, then at every fourth beat of the pendulum a stroke of a little bell is heard, thus marking the Principal Accent; if pushed in to 3, then the stroke of the bell is heard at each third beat of the pendulum, marking the Principal Accent; in this case the time is Triple; and so on.

81. Before closing this chapter it may be well to note one or two important deviations from the laws of Accent and Time, but to thoroughly understand these it is absolutely necessary that Arts. 73—77 shall have been mastered.

In the bar of $\frac{4}{4}$ time written in the margin, the first beat, the crotchet, gets the principal accent; the third beat, another crotchet, gets a secondary accent.

If we substitute a minim for the second and third crotchets, the note for the third beat (a medium accent)
will already have been sounded on the second beat (a weak accent), and is only **prolonged** into the third beat, so that it is impossible to give the accent in its proper place. The accent in such a case is given at the beginning of the note, that is, on the second beat, so that the accent is thrown back from the usual accented part of the bar to a part usually unaccented. This is called **Syncopation.**

Syncopation is an interruption of the regular flow of the accents of a tune. It occurs when a note begun on a weak accent is continued through the following stronger accent.

In the above example the minim is begun on the second beat (a weak accent) and is continued through the third beat (a medium accent); this note is said to be syncopated.

Another form in which this occurs is also given in the margin

By referring to Art. 47 for the meaning and uses of the Tie, you will see that its use here is to the effect that the crotchet at the end of the first bar is prolonged into the second bar, by the length of the crotchet to which it is tied, viz., the first crotchet in the second bar; the latter, not being sounded separately, is deprived of the accent which it would otherwise receive, and the accent is thrown back to the unaccented part, that is, to the crotchet at the end of the first bar.

In this example the syncopated note marked × is begun on the fourth beat (a weak accent), and is continued through the first beat (a strong accent) of the next bar.

Again, whenever a beat (whether strong or weak accent) consists of two or more notes, the first note has always a stronger accent than any of the succeeding notes **of that beat.** In the example given in the margin there are two notes to each of the first and second beats, therefore the first quaver in each beat has a stronger accent than the second. Now let us substitute a crotchet for the second and third quavers, thus:— (a) (b)

Then the accent, which belonged to the third quaver in example (*a*), is brought back half a beat and is given to the crotchet marked + in example (*b*); this latter note is said to be syncopated.

Notice that the syncopated note is **begun** on the **weak** half of the first beat, and is continued through the strong half of the second beat.

In the following bars, a cross is placed above the syncopated notes.

Neither of the following Rhythms contains examples of syncopation, as the continued notes do not fulfil the conditions laid down in the previous paragraphs.

82. Sometimes **three** notes of equal length are grouped together and marked ⌢3; this indicates that the three are to be sung or played in the time usually given to **two** of such notes, as in the example here given, in which the three quavers are to be sung or played in the time of two quavers or  one crotchet. Such a group of notes is called a **Triplet**. In other words, the Triplet consists of a beat divided into thirds. The student will see on referring to Art. 44 that although there are notes to represent the **half** or **quarter** or **eighth** part of a beat (whatever the beat note may

be), there is nothing to represent a **third** of a beat **in simple time**. When the music requires these thirds the only way of writing them is to make use of the sign for half a beat with the figure $\overset{3}{\frown}$ as in the above example, where the crotchet is value for a beat.

Other examples of triplets are seen in the following:—

    where each note equals one-third of a breve, or of two semibreves.

    where each note equals one-third of a semibreve, or of two minims.

    where each note equals one-third of a minim, or of two crotchets.

    where each note equals one-third of a crotchet, or of two quavers.

    where each note equals one-third of a quaver, or of two semiquavers.

    where each note equals one-third of a semiquaver, or of two demisemiquavers.

CHAPTER III.

Scales and Scale Formation.

Sharps, Flats, and Naturals. Intervals.

83. The word **Scale**, as used in Music, is derived from the Latin **scala**, meaning a **ladder**.

A **Scale** is a succession of eight musical sounds rising **in pitch** one above the other according to certain laws, somewhat like the steps of a ladder.

In a ladder the distance between any one step and the next above it or below it is the same at all parts of the ladder. It is not so in the Scale. There are greater and less distances. The greater are all equal among themselves; the less are all equal among themselves. One of the greater is double one of the smaller distances.

The small ladder with eight steps, given in the margin, is intended to represent a scale, the eight lines representing the eight sounds of the scale, and the seven spaces included between these lines, representing the distances between the sounds.

The smaller distances occur between the third and fourth, and between the seventh and eighth notes; the greater distance between any other two consecutive notes of the scale.

84. The greater distances are called in musical language **Tones.** The smaller distances are called **Semitones.**

I shall in future use the word **Interval** instead of distance.

An **Interval** is the difference in pitch (see Art. 41) between any two musical sounds. The name **interval** is also given to the difference in position, higher or lower, between any two notes on the staff.

85. To say that a **tone** is the interval between the first and second, or between the second and third, or fourth and fifth, or fifth and sixth, or sixth and seventh notes of a scale, and that a **semitone** is the interval between the third and fourth, or between the seventh and eighth notes of a scale, is, no doubt, telling you something very useful, and very necessary to be known, but it does not tell you what a tone is, or what a semitone is.

It is impossible to tell it to you in writing; it is impossible to tell it to you in words, even when oral lessons are possible. To understand what a tone or semitone is, you must hear a scale sung, or played on an instrument, and when, through your sense of hearing, your mind has realised the difference in pitch between the first and second notes of the scale, and when you have realised that it is the same as the difference between the second and third, fourth and fifth, &c., **you will know what a tone is.**

When, through your sense of hearing, your mind has realised the difference in pitch between the third and fourth notes of the scale, observed that it is the same as between the seventh and eighth, and when you have contrasted this with what we have already called a tone, **you will know what a semitone is.**

86. On examining the intervals between all the successive notes of the scale we find five tones and two semitones.

From the first note to the fourth note of the scale, both inclusive, there are three intervals, and these are respectively **tone, tone, semitone.** These **four** notes form what is called a **Tetrachord**, from two Greek words: τέτρα, four; and χορδή (not a note, but), a string which when caused to vibrate produces a note.

From the fifth to the eighth notes of a scale, both inclusive, we also have four notes with three intervals between, the intervals coming again in the same order, viz., **tone, tone, semitone;** these four notes form another tetrachord. So that a scale may be said to be made up of two tetrachords, with an interval of a tone between the two, viz., the interval from the fourth to the fifth notes of the scale.

These two tetrachords are called respectively the **Lower** and the **Upper Tetrachord**, or the **First** and the **Second** Tetrachords respectively.

87. Now look at the keyboard of a piano, harmonium, or organ. A representation of two octaves of a keyboard is given on p. 49. The keys are named in the same manner as are the musical sounds, viz., C, D, E, F, G, A, B, C. **(See Art. 10.)**

Beginning on C and touching only the white keys till you reach C, an octave above where you began, you play a scale, that is—

From C to D there is an interval of a tone
" D " E " " " "
" E " F " " " semitone
" F " G " " " tone
" G " A " " " "
" A " B " " " "
" B " C " " " semitone

and that completes the scale. The strings of the instrument are so arranged that the tones and semitones of the scale are produced in the order given above. This scale beginning on C is called the **Common Scale.**

88. In this **Common Scale** each note bears a certain fixed and known relation to the first, and also to each of the others in the scale.

It would be very monotonous to begin every piece of music on C, so for the sake of variety and the charm which it affords, we as often begin on some other note; and if we do begin on any other note, following it by notes having the same relation to each other, and to the first note, as in the Common Scale, we are said to form a New Scale on the same plan as the Common Scale.

89. If we begin with D on the keyboard of the piano or other instrument, and touch only the white keys, would we get such a scale? Let us try.

The notes would be D E F G A B C D
1 2 3 4 5 6 7 8

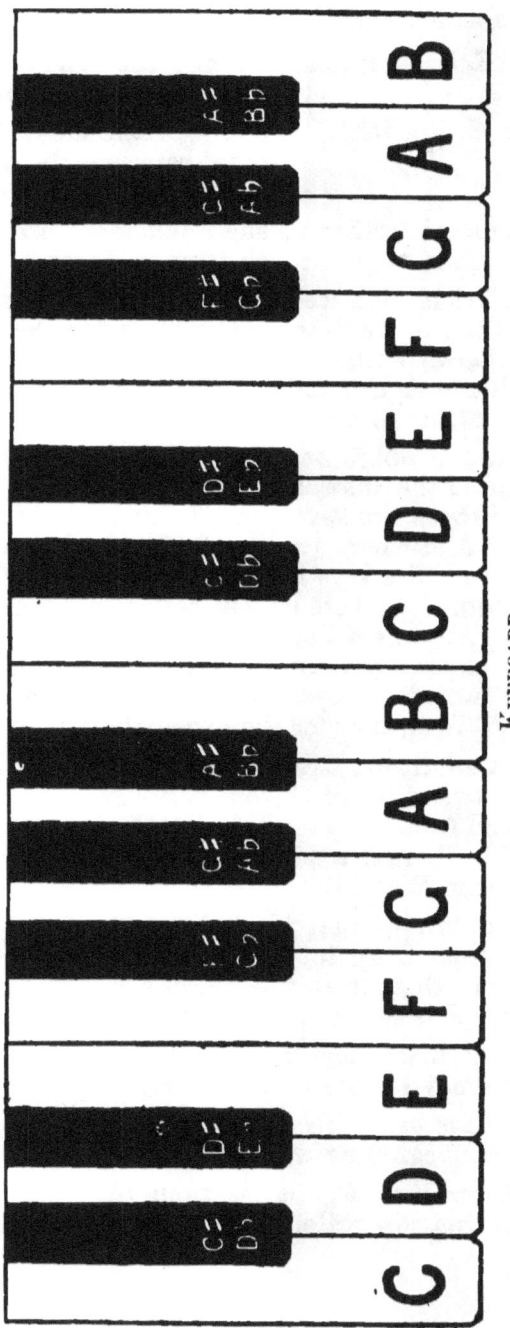

KEYBOARD.

From D_1 to E_2 is a tone. (Right.)

From E_2 to F_3 is a semitone. (Wrong; there should be a tone between the second and third.)

From F_3 to G_4 is a tone. (Wrong; there should be a semitone between the third and fourth),

and if we proceed farther we shall find more errors; it is worth your while to go through it up to D.

By other trials also we find that if we begin on any other note than C, we cannot get a scale like the Common Scale, that is, with semitones between the third and fourth and seventh and eighth notes, with tones everywhere else, **unless we alter some of the notes.**

90. **And can notes be altered?** Yes. How? Observe the keyboard of the instrument again; hitherto we have only noticed the white keys. Are there any others? Yes, black keys. And where are they? Almost between every two successive white keys there is a black key. Yes, but you said **almost.** Where do you notice that there are no black keys. Anywhere that E and F occur, or B and C, there is no black key between, but there is one between every other two white keys. Do you know the reason of that? No. Well, now for the explanation.

There is a **semitone** between E and F; there is also a **semitone** between B and C; but between C and D there is a **tone**, and from C up to that black key immediately to the right of it, there is a **semitone**, just the same interval there is between B and C.

From D **down** to that black key immediately to the left of it, or from D **up** to that black key immediately to the **right** of it, there is an interval of a **semitone**, just the same as there is between E and F, or between B and C.

Hence these black keys enable us to find a semitone anywhere we may require it in the formation of scales.

Could we have used this information in Art. 89 trying to form a scale beginning with D? Yes.

How? From E to F, that is from the second to the third note of this new scale, there is only a semitone, but this should be a tone. Now, if we take the black note to the right of F instead of the F we have taken, the interval would be a tone, which would be correct. Moreover, from the black note just named up to G, that is from the third note of this scale to the fourth, would be a semitone, which is correct also, so that we would have corrected the two errors found in Art. 89 by making that one alteration, and the lower tetrachord of that scale would have been perfectly correct.

We shall soon try again to form some new scales, profiting by this information, but it is necessary first to learn the meaning of a few new terms, and a few new symbols which must be used.

91. We have called the white keys on the keyboard of the instrument C D E F G A B C D E F G A B C, &c., repeating the names as often as there are octaves on the instrument, but we have given no names to the black keys.

Let us now supply the omission. Observe that black key immediately to the right of F; we said it is **higher** than F by a semitone; then that black key is called F **sharp.** Similarly, the black key immediately to the right of G, that is a semitone above it, is called G **sharp,** and so on with each of the others; so that we may have F **sharp,** G **sharp,** A **sharp,** C **sharp,** D **sharp,** and a little farther on we shall even speak of B **sharp,** and of E **sharp.**

92. Again, observe the black key **below,** that is to the left of D; that, we said, is a semitone lower than D; that may also be called D **flat,** though we called it by another name in Art. 91. Did we not? Yes, we called it C **sharp.** Very well then, that same key which is called C **sharp,** when we speak of it as being a semitone **above** C, is also called D **flat** when we speak of it as being a semitone **below** D, and we speak similarly of the other black keys.

By what name would you call that black key **below,** that is, immediately to the left of E? Call it E **flat.** By what other name might it be called? D **sharp.** Yes. What may that black key **below** or immediately to the left of G be called? **G flat.** Yes. In this way we may have D **flat,** E **flat,** G **flat,** A **flat,** B **flat,** and a little farther on we shall speak of C **flat,** and of F **flat.**

93. There are certain characters which on paper indicate that of which we have been speaking in Arts. 91 and 92.

This character, ♯, called a **Sharp,** placed before a note on the staff indicates that the corresponding black key on the instrument is to be touched;  thus the note written as in the margin reads F **sharp,** and the **sharp** indicates that, not the white key F, but the black key **above** it, that is immediately to the right of it, is to be touched; and the same is the case with any other note having a sharp before it; **that is to the left of it.**

Observe carefully that on the staff a sharp is always placed **to the left** of the note to be affected by it, though in writing you may put down F ♯, G ♯, &c., with the character, instead of the word **sharp,** to the right of the letter.

94. To say that any note has been **sharpened** means that it has been **raised** half a tone.

To **indicate** that a note has been sharpened, a sharp (♯) is placed to the left of the note on the staff, the sharp being on the same line or space as the note. (See Art. 98.)

Any note may also be made doubly sharp if required, that is, it may be raised two semitones; it is not usual to write two sharps before the note for this purpose, but instead of the two sharps, the character × is placed before the note. This character is called a **Double Sharp.**

In the example given in the margin the F is made doubly sharp, that is, it is raised two semitones.

95. Any note may also be **lowered half a tone.** A note is said to be **flattened** when it is **lowered** half a tone.

If on the keyboard instead of the white key G you touch the black key below, or immediately to the left of G, you are said to play G **flat,** and similarly with other keys. (See Art. 92.)

The character that represents the lowering of a note by a semitone is called a **Flat,** and is written thus ♭; it is placed on the same line or space on the staff as the note it is intended to affect, and like the sharp it is always placed **to the left** of the note thus: which reads G **flat.**

Any note may also be made doubly flat if required, that is, it may be lowered two semitones, by inserting two flats (♭♭) before it. The two flats together are called a **Double Flat.** In the example given in the margin the G is made doubly flat, that is, it is lowered two semitones.

96. When a note is neither sharp nor flat it is said to be **natural.** No sign is needed, as a general rule, to indicate that a note is **natural,** that is to be understood unless the contrary is indicated.

Nevertheless you will learn farther on, that if in the course of a piece of Music a sharp or a flat is introduced before any note, it may affect that note more than once: it will affect the note every time that note occurs from the introduction of the sharp or flat **to the end of that bar,** and in some instances even beyond the limits of that bar.

Thus, the sharp here given affects not only the first F in the bar but the second also.

Now, suppose we do not want the second F to be affected, it is necessary to have a character to indicate that: such a character is called a **Natural**: it is written ♮, and like the sharp and flat, it is placed to the left of the note, and on the same line or space on the staff.

The **natural** ♮ indicates that a note previously marked **sharp** or double sharp is to be **lowered** half a tone, or that a note previously marked flat or double flat is to be **raise**d half a tone; its use then is to contradict the use of a flat or a sharp.

So that in the bar just written if we do not wish the second F to be affected it is necessary to put a **natural** before it as shown here.

97. Having now learned the use of the **sharp, flat,** and **natural,** we are in a position to renew the attempt made in Art. 89 to write another scale after the model of the Common Scale; but we may as well be guided by experience in trying again.

There is what is called the **natural order of scale formation**. What does this mean? It means that in forming any new scale after the model of the Common Scale, the new scale should contain the fewest possible altered notes; that is the fewest possible notes with either sharps or flats before them. Now what is the fewest possible in this case? One, of course. Yes. Then the **natural order** is to form a scale which will contain **only one note** different from those found in the scale of C, or Common Scale. How is this to be done? The following will show. You saw in Art. 86 that the second tetrachord of the scale is like the first. The intervals come thus: **tone, tone, semitone**. Now suppose we make that second tetrachord of the scale of C the first tetrachord of a new scale, then that new scale will be correct as to its first half, for the intervals will be **tone, tone, semitone**.

Let us be clear about this. In saying make the second tetrachord of the scale of C the first tetrachord of a new scale, it is necessary to fix your attention on the first note of the second tetrachord in the scale of C. What is it? G. Then what will be the first note of a new scale? G, of course. If G be the first, name all the notes in the scale? G, A, B, C, D, E, F, G.

Now fix your attention on the intervals.

From
G to A (1 to 2)	there is an interval of a			tone	Right
A „ B (2 „ 3)	„	„	„	tone	„
B „ C (3 „ 4)	„	„	„	semitone	„
C „ D (4 „ 5)	„	„	„	tone	„
D „ E (5 „ 6)	„	„	„	tone	„
E „ F (6 „ 7)	„	„	„	semitone	Wrong
F „ G (7 „ 8)	„	„	„	tone	„

How are the two errors just found to be corrected? Examine their nature first. The interval from E to F is only a semitone, and it should be a tone; it is too small, then, by a semitone. How can it be made a semitone greater? By raising the F half a tone, that is by **sharpening** the F. Now what interval is there between E and F sharp? A tone. Right. And what interval will there be between F **sharp** and G? A semitone. And is that correct between the seventh and eighth of the scale? Yes. Hence you see that in correcting one of the errors we have corrected both. So we have now a new scale like the Common Scale, with only one altered note in it. What note is that? F. Yes. And what degree of the new scale is that? What number is it in order? The **seventh.** Yes; it is necessary to fix your attention on that, you will require it later on.

98. Let us now represent the scale of C and this new scale side by side on the Treble Staff, and also on the Bass Staff.

For the purpose of being able to repeat this freely in forming other scales, it is necessary to fix well in your mind that you take the **fifth** note of the scale of C as the **first** of a new scale; that only one note in the new scale then requires alteration, that note is the **seventh**, and the nature of the alteration is that it is **sharpened.**

If we now take the fifth note of the scale of G, that is D, and write from D up to its octave, sharpening the seventh note, we get a new scale, like that of either C or G. The following shows the scales of G and D side by side.

Here in the scale of D, the third note, F **sharp**, is nothing new; you see you had F **sharp** in the scale of G; see the note on fifth line; so that the seventh note, C **sharp**, is the only new note.

The following shows the formation of a new scale from the scale of D.

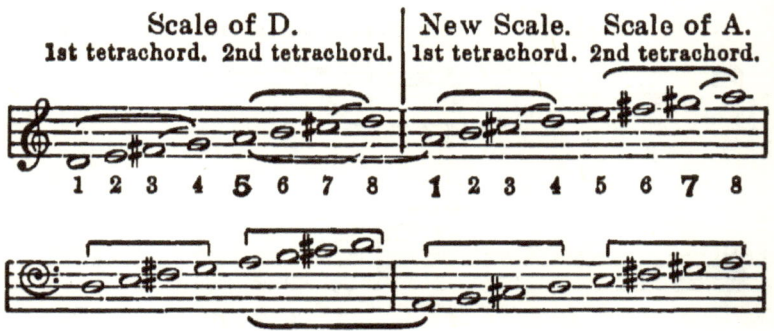

The following shows the formation of a new scale from the scale of A.

The following shows the formation of a new scale from the scale of E.

The following shows the formation of a new scale from the scale of B.

Observe that when the scale of F♯ is written on the staff as it is here with the necessary sharps before the notes, and *not as a signature* (see Art. 101), there appears to be **seven** sharps, because the first and last note being F, each must have a sharp before it, but when these are all written as a signature **six** sharps are sufficient. (See examples in Art. 99.)

Observe that as the fifth note in the scale of B is F **sharp**, so the first note of the new scale is not F, but F **sharp**.

The following shows the formation of a new scale from the scale of F **sharp**.

Observe that when the scale of C♯ is written on the staff as it is here, with the necessary sharps before the notes, and *not as a signature* (see Art. 101), there appear to be **eight** sharps, because the first and last notes being C, each requires a sharp before it, but when these are all written in a signature **seven** sharps are sufficient. (See examples in Art. 99.)

99. The Natural Order of Scale Formation leads us, as you have seen in Art. 98, to take the fifth note of any scale as the first note of a new scale, and to make **sharp** the seventh note of the new scale. Scales are thus said to **ascend by fifths**, because the **first** note of each new scale is the fifth of the preceding scale. But in reality, this is only half the natural order of scale formation, for each note altered, so far as we have gone, was altered by being **sharpened**; but new scales can be formed also by **flattening** certain notes, and by proceeding in the **natural order**, it is only necessary to flatten one note for each new scale. We shall defer the consideration of these, however, till we sum up what has been said in Arts. 97 and 98.

100. The scales already considered are the Common Scale, or Scale of C, and the others in the following list:—

1 Scale of C.	5 Scale of E.
2 Scale of G.	6 Scale of B.
3 Scale of D.	7 Scale of F♯
4 Scale of A.	8 Scale of C♯.

The common scale, or scale of C, requires no sharp notes.

The Scale of G requires 1 sharp, viz. F.
" " D " 2 sharps, " F and C.
" " A " 3 " " F, C and G.
" " E " 4 " " F, C, G and D.
" " B " 5 " " F, C, G, D and A.
" " F♯ " 6 " " F, C, G, D, A & E.
" " C♯ " 7 " " F, C, G, D, A, E & B.

These should be committed to memory thoroughly, and observe that each scale has all the sharp notes of the preceding scale and one more, that one being always the **seventh** of the new scale.

When writing the scales of F♯ and C♯, be careful to note that they both **begin** and **end** on a sharp note.

Every scale takes its name from its first note. Thus the scale of G means the scale whose first note is G.

The word **Key** is also used in the same sense as **Scale**; we speak of the **key** of G, or **key** of D, as well as of the **scale** of G, or **scale** of D, &c.

101. If a piece of music be in the scale of E or B, or any other scale requiring notes to be sharpened, or flattened, the sharps or flats necessary are not written here and there throughout the piece as required: they are all placed once for all at the beginning of the piece on the staff, and on the lines or spaces occupied by the notes that are to be made sharp or flat. When so placed they are called the **Key Signature** or **Scale Signature**. They are placed immediately after the clef, but before the **Time Signature**.

They are also written always in the order in which you saw in Art. 98 that they occur. Thus, F was the first sharp note, so F will always be first in any signature, no matter how many sharps may be in it. C was the second sharp found [necessary; so you will never find C in a signature without F being before it, and in any signature in which C occurs it will always be second, no matter how many others may be in the signature, and so on with each of the others.

You have learned (Art. 24) that F is the note on the **first space**, also on the **fifth line**. In which of these positions will the sharp be placed in the signature so as to affect all the notes in either position throughout the piece? Either position would do just as well as the other, but by **custom** it is invariably placed on the fifth line of the Treble Staff and the fourth line of the Bass Staff. With respect to other sharps there is a similar choice, but custom has long since decided the position. The following signatures show how the sharps are placed on lines or spaces on both the Treble and the Bass Clef, and also the order of their occurrence.

Signatures.
On Treble Clef.   On Bass Clef.

Scale of G,
one sharp, F.

Scale of D,
two sharps, F and C.

Scale of A,
three sharps,
F, C, and G.

Scale of E,
four sharps,
F, C, G, and D.

Scale of B,
five sharps,
F, C, G, D, and A.

Scale of F#,
six sharps,
F, C, G, D, A, and E.

Scale of C#,
seven sharps,
F, C, G, D, A, E, and B.

The following shows the arrangement of the sharps after the C clef, Alto and Tenor.

You should write all these frequently till you are quite familiar with the doing of it, and you should note carefully, how to place each sharp in the signature on the staff, both as to line or space on which it is to be placed, and also the order in which it is to be placed, with reference to those that precede, or follow it, or both. The order is always F, C, G, D, A, E, B; so that if there be but one, that is F; if two, they will be F and C; the F must be written first; and so on.

101a. It is necessary to be able to tell the signature of any scale or key instantly from memory; it is also necessary, seeing the signature, to be able to tell the key of which it is the signature. That is very easily done if you attend to the following:—You saw that in each new scale formed the **seventh** note was made sharp; hence the **last sharp** in each of the foregoing signatures is the **seventh** of the scale; knowing the seventh, you can easily tell the **eighth** which is the same in name as the **first**.

Applying this when the signature is one sharp F, we know that F is the **seventh** of the scale. So G must be the **eighth**, and of course G must be the **first**; so we see it is the scale of G.

If there be two sharps in the signature, they are F and C; C is the **last**; this is the **seventh** of the scale, so D must be the **eighth**, and D must be the **first**, so it is the scale of D.

If there be three sharps, they are F, C, and G; G is the **last**; so G is the **seventh** of the scale; and A must be **eighth**; so of course the first is A; this time the scale is A; and so on in other cases.

The next note above the last sharp in any signature always gives the key note.

By **Key Note** is meant the **first** note of a scale or key.

102. Now for the consideration of the formation of scales having **flats** in the key signature.

Beginning again with the scale of C. Count up, not to its fifth note this time, but to its **fourth**; $C_1 D_2 E_3 F_4$; we find F. Making F the first note of a scale, what are all the notes of the scale? F, G, A, B, C, D, E, F. Let us see if it be necessary to alter any, and if so, what notes, so as to make it like the scale of C.

From F to G (1 to 2) is a tone.	Right.	
„ G „ A (2 „ 3) „ „	„	
„ A „ B (3 „ 4) „ „	Wrong; should be a semitone, 3 to 4.	
„ B „ C (4 „ 5) „ semitone.	Wrong; should be a tone, 4 to 5.	
„ C „ D (5 „ 6) „ tone.	Right.	
„ D „ E (6 „ 7) „ „	„	
„ E „ F (7 „ 8) „ semitone.	„	

We have two errors, suggesting that alteration is necessary. The first error is between A and B, the third and fourth notes of *this* scale, which is a tone but should be only a semitone: let us correct that by flattening the B: now, from A to B **flat** is only a **semitone**: that is correct: from B **flat** to C is now a **tone**, and that is correct also between the fourth and fifth of the scale; so that in correcting one of the errors we have corrected both.

We should now have a new scale like the scale of C: let us write both side by side, on both the Treble Staff and Bass Staff.

Observe that in the new scale the second tetrachord, C, D, E, F, is the same as the first tetrachord in the scale of C.

All the notes in the new scale are the same as in the old scale except one: that one is B, the **fourth note** of the new scale, and it is altered by **flattening** it.

Similarly, if we take the fourth note of the scale of F as the first of a new scale, we can form another like the scale of C or F **by flattening the fourth note** of the new scale, and so on to other scales.

103. The following shows the formation of a new scale from that of F.

Observe that we simply take the fourth note of the old scale as the first of a new scale, and beginning on this write up to its octave, making the **fourth note** flat in the new scale.

The following shows the formation of a new scale from that of B♭.

The following shows the formation of a new scale from that of E♭.

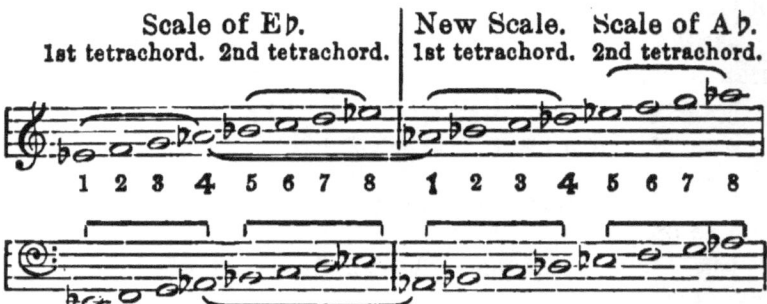

The following shows the formation of a new scale from that of A♭.

The following shows the formation of a new scale from that of D♭.

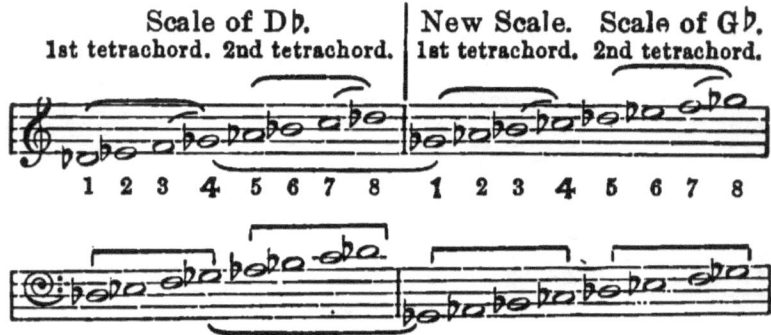

The following shows the formation of a new scale from that of G♭.

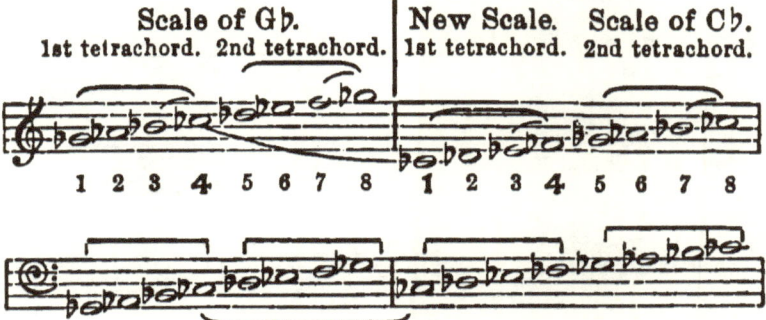

104. Art. 103 shows that the natural order of scale formation when there are to be flats in the signature is to **ascend a fourth** each time for the first note of the new scale, and to **flatten** the fourth note of the new scale; just as when there were to be **sharps** in the signature we **ascended a fifth** each time and made the seventh note sharp in each new scale.

The scales formed in Arts. 102 and 103 are in order of formation, C, F, B♭, E♭, A♭, D♭, G♭ and C♭. We also say that Scale of F requires 1 flat, B.

```
     "     B♭   "   2 flats, B and E.
     "     E♭   "   3   "    B, E and A.
     "     A♭   "   4   "    B, E, A and D.
     "     D♭   "   5   "    B, E, A, D and G.
     "     G♭   "   6   "    B, E, A, D, G and C.
     "     C♭   "   7   "    B, E, A, D, G, C and F.
```

As in the case of the sharps, the flats are also always written in the key signature in the above order; B always comes first, E second, A third, D fourth, and so on, no matter how many flats there may be in the signature.

It is very important to note this carefully.

Note also that the scales of B♭, E♭, A♭, D♭, G♭ and C♭ both *begin* and *end* with a flat note.

F

105. The following exhibits the key signatures in flats, with their correct placing on the lines and spaces of both the Treble and the Bass Clef.

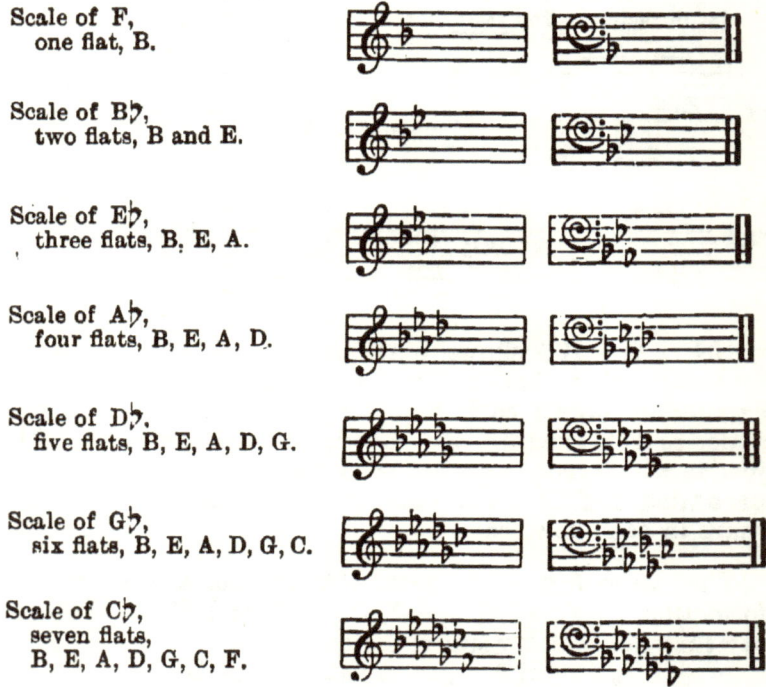

Scale of F, one flat, B.

Scale of B♭, two flats, B and E.

Scale of E♭, three flats, B, E, A.

Scale of A♭, four flats, B, E, A, D.

Scale of D♭, five flats, B, E, A, D, G.

Scale of G♭, six flats, B, E, A, D, G, C.

Scale of C♭, seven flats, B, E, A, D, G, C, F.

The following shows the arrangement of the flats after the C clef, Alto and Tenor.

Alto   Tenor

It is necessary to commit the above to memory.

Observe that when any scale, **beginning** and **ending** with a flat note, is written on a staff, with the necessary flats before the notes, and **not written as a signature**, there will **appear** to be one more flat than is shown in the signatures here. That is in consequence of the flat which is used for the **first** note being **repeated** in a **different** position on the staff for the **eighth** note.

105a. If you see a signature in flats, and you want to tell of what key it is the signature, bear in mind you saw that the **last flat** is always the fourth note of the key, so that if the signature be five flats, B, E, A, D, G, you see G is the **last flat,** that is the fourth note of the scale; so count down four from G, thus:—G_1, F_2, E_3, D_4; the scale is D **flat.**

A fourth below the last flat in the key signature always gives the keynote.

106. A **Diatonic** Scale is one in which the progression from note to note is **chiefly** by tones, and when not by tones, then by semitones. The term is derived from two Greek words, **dia** through, and **tonos** a tone.

All the scales we have already considered are examples of Diatonic Scales.

The scales already considered are also called **Major Scales,** and the name suggests what is in reality a fact, viz., that there is another class called **Minor Scales.**

Why these names are given to them, and what the distinction is between a Major and a Minor Scale, cannot very well be explained until you have studied the subject of intervals, on which we now enter. Having studied that, see Arts. 126 and 127.

CHAPTER IV.

Intervals, their Kind and Quality.

107. An **Interval** is the difference in pitch between any two musical sounds; or the difference in **position** on the staff between any two notes.

Hitherto we have only considered the intervals between two **consecutive** notes of a scale, as for example, the interval between C and D, or between D and E. But we may consider the interval from C to F, or C to G, or from D to A, or D to C, and so on; so that we may expect to find on examination that there are **different kinds of intervals.**

It will tend to brevity later on to remark here that if we speak of the interval from C to G : C and G are called **The Extremes of the Interval**, that is they are the two outside notes including the interval, the one being at the lower end and the other at the upper end of the interval.

If we speak of the interval B to D, then B and D are called the **Extremes of the Interval.**

If we speak of the interval F to B, then F and B are called the **Extremes of the Interval.**

108. The **Kinds of Interval** take their names from the number of notes on the staff, from the lower extreme of the interval to the upper extreme, **both extremes being counted.**

Thus, speaking of the interval C to D, count thus: C_1, D_2; this interval is called a **Second.** (See example in Art. 109.)

C to E, count thus: C_1, D_2, E_3; this is a **Third**. (See examples in Art. 110.)

C to F, count thus: C_1, D_2, E_3, F_4; this is a **Fourth**. (See examples in Art. 111.)

G to D, count thus: G_1, A_2, B_3, C_4, D_5; this is a **Fifth**. (See examples in Art. 112.)

A to F, count thus: A_1, B_2, C_3, D_4, E_5, F_6; this is a **Sixth**. (See examples in Art. 114.)

B to A, count thus: B_1, C_2, D_3, E_4, F_5, G_6, A_7; this is a **Seventh**. (See examples in Art. 115.)

D to D: this is an **Octave**. (See example in Art. 113.)

You will soon come to be so familiar with counting that you will find this method altogether too slow and irksome; a much quicker method of counting is that given in Art. 183 on Chords, if you omit the eighth note and count the seventh in its place, thus:—

1	3	5	7
C	E	G	B
D	F	A	C
E	G	B	D
F	A	C	E
G	B	D	F
A	C	E	G
B	D	F	A

You will thus know the third, fifth, and seventh from any note at a glance, and from the third to the fourth, or from the fifth to the sixth, you can easily pass if necessary.

Hence we see that the **kinds** of interval are Seconds, Thirds, Fourths, Fifths, Sixths, Sevenths, and Octaves.

The name **Unison** is given to the interval between two notes of the **same pitch**, and placed on the same line or space on the staff.

Observe carefully that whenever an interval is named as D to C the **first-named note** is to be taken as the **lower extreme** of the interval, and you are to count from that to the upper one, thus D_1, E_2, F_3, G_4, A_5, B_6, C_7.

You are not to say **C** to **D**, this is a Second, when you are asked about **D** to **C**; the one is what is called the **Inversion** of the other, but they are very unlike, both in name and in nature, so be careful not to confound them.

What kind is the interval E to A? E_1, F_2, G_3, A_4. This is a fourth. Yes, that is right.

109. Intervals **of the same kind** may differ in **quality**; the **quality** depending upon the number of tones or semitones the interval contains. One interval may be larger or smaller than another **of the same kind**.

The **Value of an Interval** is a term used herein to mean the number of tones or semitones contained in the interval.

Thus C to D is a **Second**. What is its value? One tone.
    D „ E   „   „   „   One tone.
    E „ F   „   „   „   One semitone.

Here, then, the interval E to F, though of the same **kind** as the interval C to D, is not of the same **quality**.

The interval E to F is **smaller**; the interval C to D, or D to E, is **greater**; hence the interval C to D, or D to E, is called a **Major Second**; the interval E to F, or B to C, is called a **Minor Second.**

The following shows an interval of a second on each

note in the scale of C; two open notes are used when the interval is Major; one open and one closed black note when the interval is Minor. You will observe that the first, second, fourth, fifth and sixth notes of the scale bear Major Seconds, while the third and seventh bear Minor Seconds.

Observe this use of the word **bear**; no further definition of the term will be given.

You should now write some of the other Major Scales given in Arts. 98 and 103, and if you form an interval of a Second upon each note of any one of them, you will find these Seconds agree **in quality** with the corresponding ones given above; thus the fourth note of any Major Scale will bear a Major Second; the third or the seventh will bear a Minor Second, and so on. (See Art. 127 for meaning of Major Scale.)

110. The following shows an interval of a Third formed on each note in the scale of C; C to E contains two tones, D to F contains one tone and one semitone:

1 2 3 4 5 6 7

These differ **in quality**, the former is called a Major Third, the latter a Minor Third. The Major Thirds are distinguished in the example by two open notes; the Minor Thirds by one open note and a black note; you should count each carefully and see that what is here stated concerning it is correct.

Write any other Major Scale; form a Third on each note of it, and on counting the value of each carefully you will find that the same degrees of both scales bear Thirds of the same quality; for instance the sixth note of the scale given above bears a Minor Third; the sixth of any other Major Scale will also bear a Minor Third; test it. (See Art. 127 for meaning of Major Scale.)

111. The **qualities** of Interval so far are **Major** and **Minor**, and they apply to Seconds, Thirds, Sixths and Sevenths. In speaking of Fourths and Fifths, the terms **Perfect, Augmented** and **Diminished** are used to express difference of quality, though other terms equally good have been used for the same purpose.

The following shows a Fourth written on each degree of the scale of C; C to F contains **two tones and a half**, that is called a Perfect Fourth, and it will be observed that each note in the scale bears a Perfect Fourth except one, that is the Fourth note of the scale, F:—

1 2 3 4 5 6 7

F to G is one tone; G to A is one tone; A to B is one tone; so that F to B is three tones; this is called an **Augmented Fourth**, or from the fact that its value is **three** tones it is called a **Tritone** Fourth.

It is remarkable, and you should bear in mind that only one such interval occurs in any scale, and that it occurs on the Fourth note in the scale.

Here you should write some other Major Scale, form a Fourth on each note, and see that the **quality** of the Fourth corresponds with that of the fourth on the same degree of the scale given above. (See Art. 127 for meaning of Major Scale.)

112. The following shows a Fifth written on each note of the scale of C: counting the first one, C to G, we find three tones and one semitone, viz., C to D a tone; D to E a tone; E to F a semitone; F to G a tone; total, three tones and a semitone. This is called a **Perfect Fifth**. Each note in the scale bears a Perfect Fifth, except the **seventh** which bears a **Diminished Fifth**, value **two tones and two semitones**:

Write any other Major Scale; form a Fifth on each note, and you will find the qualities to correspond with those just given.

Note carefully that only one Diminished Fifth occurs in any scale, and that it is found on the seventh of the scale.

113. All Octaves are **Perfect**, the value of each being five tones and two semitones:

114. As in the case of Seconds and Thirds, the qualities of Sixths and Sevenths are Major and Minor.

The following shows a Sixth written on each note of the scale of C. Counting the first one, C to A, we find it contains four tones and one semitone, that is a **Major**

Sixth. Counting the Sixth on E, the third note of the scale, we find it contains three tones and two semitones; that is a **Minor Sixth.**

The Major and Minor Intervals are indicated in the usual way above.

If you write any other Major Scale, and write a Sixth on each note of it, you will find that on the corresponding degrees of the scale the **quality** of the Sixth will correspond with what is given above.

115. The following shows a Seventh formed on each note of the scale of C, with the Major and Minor indicated in the usual way. On counting, it is found that the Major contains five tones and one semitone; the Minor contains four tones and two semitones:

If any other Major Scale be written and a Seventh be formed on each note, it will be found that the quality of any Seventh will correspond with that of the Seventh on the corresponding degree of the scale given above.

116. Summary to be committed to memory.
Value of a Major Second, one tone.
    „   Minor Second, one semitone.
    „   Major Third, two tones.
    „   Minor Third, one tone and one semitone.
    „   Perfect Fourth, two tones and one semitone.
    „   Augmented Fourth } three tones.
           or Tritone Fourth
    „   Perfect Fifth, three tones and one semitone.
    „   Diminished Fifth, two tones and two semitones.
    „   Major Sixth, four tones and one semitone.
    „   Minor Sixth, three tones and two semitones.
    „   Major Seventh, five tones and one semitone.
    „   Minor Seventh, four tones and two semitones.
    „   Perfect Octave, five tones and two semitones.

Typical examples of intervals—all taken from the scale of C.

C to D, Major Second.   E to F, Minor Second.
C to E, Major Third.   E to G, Minor Third.
C to F, Perfect Fourth.   F to B, Augmented Fourth.
C to G, Perfect Fifth.   B to F, Diminished Fifth.
C to A, Major Sixth.   E to C, Minor Sixth.
C to B, Major Seventh.   E to D, Minor Seventh.
C to C, Perfect Octave.   E to E, Perfect Octave.

117. How to tell the Kind and Quality of an interval.

Suppose you are asked what interval is this, G to C♯?  Proceed thus: count the number of notes from the lower extreme to the upper, **both included**, thus G_1, A_2, B_3, C_4. It is a **Fourth**. That is the **kind** of interval, and always settle the **kind** first.

Now for the **quality**. Count the number of tones and semitones from the lower extreme to the upper, thus:

G to A is one tone.
A to B is one tone.
B to C♯ is one tone.

Altogether from G to C♯ there are three tones.

Now we know, not only that the interval is a Fourth, but that there are three tones in it. What quality is it? Reference to Arts. 111 and 116, which you should have thoroughly committed to memory, shows that it is an **Augmented** Fourth, or **Tritone** Fourth.

One example more. What interval is this, A to E♭?

Count A_1, B_2, C_3, D_4, E_5. It is a **Fifth**.
Count again, A to B is one tone.
    „   B „ C „ one semitone.
    „   C „ D „ one tone.
    „   D „ E♭ „ one semitone.

So that A to E♭ contains two tones and two semitones.

Referring to Arts. 112 and 116, this is seen to be a **Diminished** Fifth.

If you follow this plan carefully you will never have a mistake in telling either the **kind** or **quality** of an interval, and if you give yourself reasonable practice at it, you will find that you can soon go through it with great rapidity.

Either of the foregoing questions should be answered leisurely **in less than two seconds,** and especially when you begin to adopt the method of counting in Arts. 183 and 108.

118. How to form an interval of given Kind and Quality on a given note.

Example: Form a Diminished Fifth on D.

Proceed thus: The interval is to be a Fifth (**kind** first). Count D_1, E_2, F_3, G_4, A_5. A forms a Fifth with D. Write down A above the D.

Now, by Art. 116 a Diminished Fifth contains two tones and two semitones. Count and see what is the value of the interval D to A, as written.

> D to E is one tone.
> E to F is one semitone.
> F to G is one tone.
> G to A is one tone.

So that D to A is three tones and one semitone. That is a Perfect Fifth. It must be made smaller, but **without altering the position of either note.**

There are two ways of making an interval smaller:—

(a) by lowering the upper extreme,
(b) by raising the lower extreme.

In this case, as the lower extreme is the given note D, **it must not be altered in any way,** so we are simply left to lower the upper extreme. Put a flat before A. D to A ♭ is the required interval.

One example more. Write a Major Sixth on F♯. Count F_1, G_2, A_3, B_4, C_5, D_6.

D forms a Sixth with F;
set down D **above** F♯. Now
by Art. 116 a **Major** Sixth
contains four tones and one semitone.

So count again, F♯ to G is one semitone.
          G to A is one tone.
          A to B is one tone.
          B to C is one semitone.
          C to D is one tone.

Here we have three tones and two semitones from F♯ to D. But that is a Minor Sixth. This must be made greater, **but without altering the position of either note.**

There are two ways of making an interval greater:—

    (*a*) by raising the upper extreme,
    (*b*) by lowering the lower extreme.

In this case as the lower extreme is **the given note F♯, it must not be altered in any way,** so we are simply left to raise the upper extreme.

Raise the upper extreme a semitone by putting a sharp before the D, and we get the interval F♯ to D♯ as the Major Sixth required.

You need not show on paper at examination the three steps given in this Art., but you require to go through the three **mentally**, and with a fair share of practice you will be able to do so rapidly.

In less than two seconds either of the foregoing questions should be answered if you have Art. 116 committed to memory.

119. You learned that the effect of a flat (♭) is to lower a note by a semitone.

The effect of a double flat (♭♭) is to lower a note two semitones.

A sharp (♯) raises a note a semitone.

A double sharp (×) raises a note two semitones.

If a note be made **doubly flat,** and it is required to remove the effect of one of the flats, the flat is removed and a **natural** is put in its place, thus ♮♭. Similarly, if a note has been made doubly sharp, and we want it singly sharp, insert a natural and one sharp, thus ♮♯.

120. All the intervals named in Art. 116 are found **naturally** in any of the scales named in Arts. 98 to 103; but as you have learned the use of **a sharp, a flat, a double sharp,** and **a double flat,** you will easily understand that the **quality** of any interval named in Art. 116 may be altered by the introduction of any one of those characters not already placed before either or both extremes of the interval.

For example, take the Second, G to A; this is a Major Second; but we may make it greater, either  by placing a ♯ before the A, or by placing a ♭ before the G. In either case it becomes a semitone greater than a Major Second.

It is then called an **Augmented** Second. Its value is one tone and a half: that is **equal** to a Minor Third, **but you must not on that account call it a Minor Third.**

The value of an interval only determines its **quality,** not its **kind.** (See Art. 108.)

Again, take the interval G to D, that is a perfect Fifth. Augment it by raising the D a semitone; now it is a semitone more than a Perfect Fifth, it is an **Augmented** Fifth.

Or take the interval D♭ to B♭: that is a Major Sixth. Augment it by raising the B♭: this is done by removing the ♭ and inserting a ♮ in its place. The interval is now a semitone more than a Major Sixth. It is now an **Augmented** Sixth.

121. An **Augmented Interval** is one a semitone greater than a Major or Perfect Interval **of the same kind.**

Any interval may be augmented, as indicated above, but the only Augmented Intervals used in musical composition are Seconds, Fourths, Fifths, Sixths and Octaves. The reason of this belongs to a study of the Laws of Harmony.

122. Take the Minor Third, A to C; this may be made smaller either by lowering the  C a semitone, that is, by inserting a ♭ before it; or by raising the A a semitone, that is, by inserting a ♯ before it. In either case the interval is made a semitone less than a Minor Third. It is then called a **Diminished** Third.

Or take the Perfect Fourth, A to D; **diminish** it, either by inserting a ♭ before D, or by inserting a ♯ before A. In 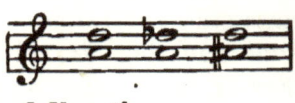 either case it becomes a **Diminished** Fourth.

Or take the Minor Seventh, E to D; **diminish** it, either by inserting a ♯ before E, or by in-  serting a ♭ before D. In either case it becomes a semitone less than a Minor Seventh. It is then a **Diminished** Seventh.

123. A **Diminished Interval** is one a semitone less than a Minor Interval **of the same kind.** But in the case of Fourths, Fifths, and Octaves, an interval a semitone less than a Perfect is called a **Diminished** Interval.

Any interval may be **diminished** in the manner shown in the examples given in Art. 122, but the only Diminished Intervals found in musical compositions are Thirds, Fourths, Fifths, Sevenths, and Octaves. The reason for this belongs to the study of the Laws of Harmony.

124. Arts. 117 and 118 should now be carefully re-studied in connection with Arts. 120–123, and Art. 116.

125. All the intervals found **naturally** in any Diatonic Scale are called **Diatonic Intervals.**

Intervals formed by the introduction of flats or sharps not belonging to a Key Signature are called **Chromatic Intervals.**

In any scale there cannot be any particular note, **natural, and** the same note either **flat or sharp.** From any note natural, to the same note sharp or flat, is an interval of a semitone, and as this must be formed by the introduction of a sharp or a flat not belonging to the Key Signature, this is a Chromatic Interval.

Hence the interval from any note to the same note either sharp or flat is a **Chromatic Semitone.**

The semitones which occur naturally in a scale, as between the third and fourth, or seventh and eighth of a Major Scale are called **Diatonic Semitones.**

The alteration of any note in a scale by inserting a flat or a sharp before it, is called a **Chromatic Alteration** of the note.

If in any ascending Major Scale we chromatically raise the notes as required, so as to proceed all the way by semitones; and if in descending we chromatically lower the notes of the Major Scale as required, so as to proceed by semitones all the way, we are said to form a **Chromatic Scale.**

The following is an example of a Chromatic Scale:—

It is more usual, however, in the ascending scale, instead of chromatically raising the sixth note, to chromatically lower the seventh in the ascending scale: and in the descending scale, instead of the lowered fifth, it is usual to write the raised fourth.

The reason for this cannot be explained in an elementary book, further than to say that though we are so far considering A♯ and B♭ to be the same, and F♯ and G♭ to be the same note, they are not exactly so in reality, and in the places just referred to, the B♭ and the F♯ are the truer notes.

With this alteration then, the following is the form of Chromatic Scale mostly used:—

125a. The following is a list of all the intervals used in Music :—

I.—Found in the Major Scale :—

No. of examples in each Scale.

Perfect Unison	Seven.
Major Second	Five.
Minor Second	Two.
Major Third	Three.
Minor Third	Four.
Perfect Fourth	Six.
Augmented Fourth	One.
Perfect Fifth	Six.
Diminished Fifth	One.
Major Sixth	Four.
Minor Sixth	Three.
Major Seventh	Two.
Minor Seventh	Five.
Perfect Octave	Seven.

II.—Found only in Minor Scale :—See Arts. 126 to 136.

No. of examples in each Scale.

Augmented Second	One.
Augmented Fifth	One.
Diminished Seventh	One.
Diminished Fourth	One.

III.—Borrowed from the Chromatic Scale :—
Augmented Sixth.
Diminished Third.
Chromatic Semitone or Augmented Unison.
Augmented and Diminished Octaves.

You should now verify each statement about the number of examples in each scale by taking any particular scale, say the scale of C Major, and finding the actual intervals referred to. You will be able to find the Minor Scale intervals after having studied the next chapter.

CHAPTER V.

Minor Scales.

126. We have already seen (Art. 86) that the order of tones in a tetrachord is **tone, tone, semitone;** we have seen also that the tetrachord is so called because of its containing **four notes,** and not because of the position of the semitone with respect to the tones.

It would still be a tetrachord if the semitone came first, or if it came between the two tones.

If the semitone came first, what would be the value of the whole interval **from the first to the third** note of the tetrachord? It would be one tone and one semitone.

If the semitone came second, that is between the two tones, what would be the value of the whole interval **from the first to the third** note of the tetrachord? Again, it would be one tone and one semitone.

And what **kind** of interval is it **from the first to the third?** A third, of course.

And what **quality** is that third so long as its value is one tone and one semitone? A **Minor** Third.

But when the semitone comes last, as in Art. 86, what then is the value of the interval **from the first to the third** note? Two tones.

What is the **quality** of the Third then? A **Major** Third. Then what is the **kind** and **quality** of the interval between the **first** and **third** notes of each of the scales in Arts. 98 and 108? It is a **Major Third** in each case.

For that reason, each of those scales is called a **Major Scale.**

G

127. A **Major Scale** is one in which the interval from the first to the third note of the scale is a **Major** Third.

A **Minor Scale** is one in which the interval from the first to the third note is a **Minor** Third.

There are many other points of difference between the two which you will learn further on.

128. Every Major Scale has a corresponding or **Relative Minor** Scale, that is a Minor Scale containing the **same notes** as the Major Scale, though differently arranged, so that if a note be sharp, flat, or natural, in the one, it will be so in the other also.

129. Referring to Art. 110, do you remember what notes of a Major Scale bear Minor Thirds? Yes, the second, third, sixth and seventh.

Very well, then, if we make the second, third, sixth, or seventh of **any** Major Scale the **first** of a new scale, what **quality** of third will that first bear?

A Minor Third of course! Yes.

Then if, as stated in last question, we make the second, third, sixth, or seventh of any Major Scale the first of a new scale, we obtain a Minor Scale, because the interval from its first to its third note would be a Minor Third, and if we use no notes except those used in the Major Scale, then we are said to have a **Relative** Minor to the Major.

130. It thus appears that there **might be** four relative Minors to any Major Scale. So there **might,** but **there are not,** for all that.

Out of the four **possible,** one is chosen, and only that one is used.

What one is that? The one beginning on the sixth of the Major Scale.

131. How to form the Relative Minor to any Major Scale.

Take for example the Major Scale of C.

Count the notes of the Major Scale till you come to the sixth, thus :—C_1, D_2, E_3, F_4, G_5, A_6.

Make that sixth, A, the first of a new scale, and write from A up to its octave. You have then a Minor Scale. The following shows this:—

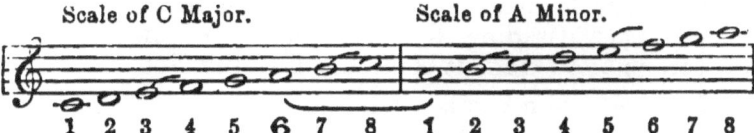

Observe that by descending a third from C we find A, just as well as by ascending a sixth.

Nothing could be much simpler than that, but having found out this, it is to be observed that this is **only one** of the forms of Minor Scale, and that it is now almost obsolete, if not indeed entirely so, as to the ascending half of it.

However, as it forms a good foundation for the others we will give it some consideration. You see there are five tones and two semitones in it, but the semitones are between the **second** and **third, fifth** and **sixth** notes.

There is not a semitone between the seventh and eighth as in the Major Scale, and as the ear naturally desires to hear a semitone there, the above form of Minor Scale was altered so as to provide a semitone from the seventh to the eighth.

This first form of Minor Scale is called the **Unaltered Form,** because no note in it is altered from what it was in the Major Scale.

It is also called the **Diatonic Form,** for the same reason that the Major Scale is called Diatonic. (See Art. 106.)

132. The seventh note of a scale **leading** on to the eighth by the small interval of a semitone is called a **Leading Note.** The Leading Note is very peculiar in its nature; once sounded, it suggests that something else is to follow, and it creates the desire to hear that something, and that desire is not satisfied till you hear the eighth after the seventh.

This can be but very poorly expressed in words; you must hear someone sing or play a scale, or do so yourself up to the seventh, the Leading Note, and leave off there if you can; then you will realise what has just been but faintly described.

133. The form of Minor Scale given in Art. 131 not containing a Leading Note, it was found necessary to alter it, so as to make it contain a Leading Note.

This was not difficult; all that was necessary was to raise the seventh, so as to bring it a semitone nearer the eighth; when that is done, there is only a semitone between the seventh and eighth. The seventh is then a Leading Note.

The following shows the ascending half of the scale in Art. 131 written with the raised seventh. This is called the **Harmonic** Form of Minor Scale. It is also called the **Chromatic** Form, for the reason given in Art. 134.

Note that there are now three semitones in the scale, viz., between **two** and **three, five** and **six, seven** and **eight,** and the scale **is the same in descending** as in ascending.

134. Even the form of Minor Scale in Art. 133 has not been found altogether satisfactory, on account of the disagreeable Chromatic Interval, an Augmented Second, now existing between the sixth and seventh notes of the scale, that is, between F and G ♯.

To avoid this disagreeable interval, this form of Minor Scale has been further altered, by **raising the sixth** as well as the seventh. The following shows the raised sixth and raised seventh:—

You will see that now there is no Augmented Second: and there are only two semitones, viz., between **two and three,** and **seven** and **eight.**

The ear does not so much desire to hear the Leading Note in the descending scale as in the ascending, and hence when **both** the sixth and seventh are raised in the ascending scale they are both lowered again in the descending scale. The above, then, does not show this form of Minor Scale fully. The following shows it both ascending and descending, the sixth and seventh being lowered again in descending :—

This is called the **Melodic** Form of Minor Scale.

It is also called the **Altered Diatonic Form,** because it is Diatonic in the same sense as the Major Scale is Diatonic, and some notes in it are **altered** from what they were in the Major Scale.

There is also a fourth form of Minor Scale, viz., that having the sixth and seventh raised both in the ascending and descending scale, so that in both cases **there is an interval of Major Sixth and Major Seventh respectively, from the first to the sixth and seventh notes of the scale.**

The following shows this form :—

Maj. 6th. Maj. 7th. Maj. 7th. Maj. 6th.

As another example of this form, take the following :—
Key of C ♯ Minor (fourth form).   Relative to E Major.

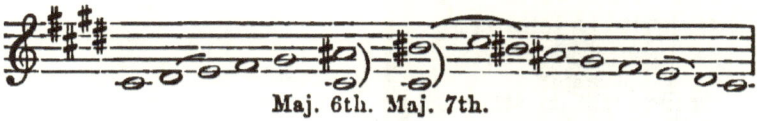

Maj. 6th. Maj. 7th.

135. After the same manner let us now proceed to write in the three forms first given the Relative Minor Scale to G Major.

First write the scale of G Major, putting the necessary sharp in the proper place for key signature at the beginning and not immediately before the F. Count G_1, A_2, B_3, C_4, D_5, E_6. We thus find that the Relative Minor is E.

Hence write as follows :—

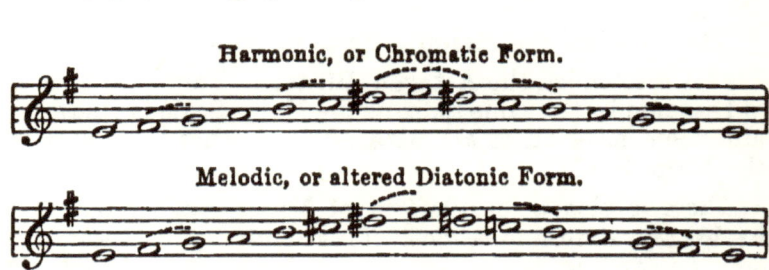

Observe carefully that the same key signature does for both the Major Scale and its Relative Minor.

You should now yourself write in three forms the Relative Minor Scales to all the Major Scales with **sharp** signatures.

One more example is given to assist you. Write the Relative Minor to E Major. Signature of E Major is four sharps, F, C, G and D. Count as before E_1, F_2, G_3, A_4, B_5, C_6. We find C is the sixth note in the scale of E Major. Whether is this C, flat, sharp, or natural? **Sharp**, of course. Then we say C♯ Minor is the relative to E Major. Hence write as follows :—

Harmonic or Chromatic Form.

Melodic, or altered Diatonic Form.

For the fourth form of this scale see Art. 184.

The following shows the scale of C Minor relative of E♭ Major in three forms:—

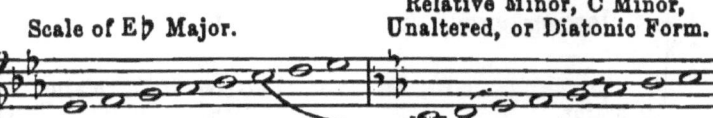

C Minor. Harmonic, or Chromatic Form.

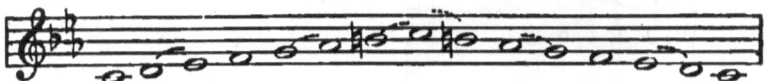

Melodic, or altered Diatonic Form.

If in the Melodic Form we retain the **naturals** in the descending scale, instead of restoring the flats, we have the fourth form mentioned in Art. 184.

Be careful not to confound the scale of C Minor with that of C **sharp** Minor already given.

The following shows three forms of D Minor, relative to F Major:—

D Minor. Harmonic or Chromatic Form.

Melodic, or altered Diatonic Form.

Observe carefully the nature of the Accidentals required to indicate the raising of the sixth and seventh in the ascending scale, and the lowering of them again in the descending scale.

The following shows three forms of G Minor relative of B♭ Major:—

B♭ Major.   G Minor, (Relative of B♭ Major). Unaltered or Diatonic Form.

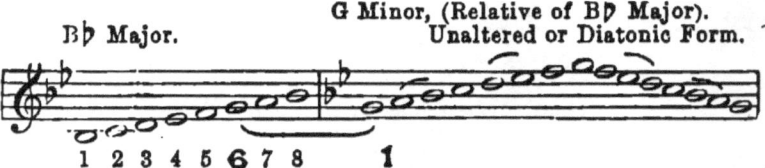

1 2 3 4 5 6 7 8   1

G Minor. Harmonic or Chromatic Form.

Melodic, or altered Diatonic Form.

Again your attention is directed to the Accidentals found necessary in the Melodic Form to raise the sixth and seventh in the ascending scale, and to lower them again in the descending scale.

The Relative Major Scale is in each case written here with the Minor for the purpose of fixing all the better in your mind the nature of the relation, but you are not expected to do it at any examination unless you are specially asked to do so.

136. The Relative Minor to A♭ Major is here written as a further example of Minor Scale with flat signature.

The signature of A♭ Major is four flats, B, E, A, and D.

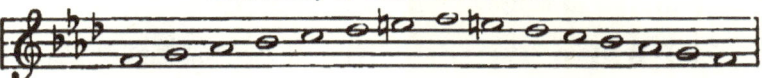

Notice that here the **raising** of the sixth and seventh is effected by inserting a ♮ in each case to contradict the ♭ in the key signature: and in the Melodic Form the **lowering** is done again by removing the ♮ and restoring the ♭ corresponding to that in the signature.

You should now yourself write in three forms the Relative Minor Scales to all the Major Scales, with **flat** signatures.

One short example more. Write the Harmonic Form (ascending half only) of the Relative Minor to C♯ Major.

The descending Melodic Form of this would be

In the ascending Harmonic Form the G is already **sharp** by the signature, when it is further raised it is made **double sharp**; hence use ×.

In the descending Melodic Form, the ♮ is used to indicate the **lowering** by taking away one of the sharps.

137. In the examinations of the Education Department the names given in Arts. 133 to 136 for the different forms of Minor Scale **are never used.**

Other expressions are used to signify the same thing; the following are some of them:—

(a) Write a Minor Scale **with a Raised Seventh.**

(b) Write a Minor Scale **with a Major Seventh.**

(c) Write a Minor Scale **with a Minor Sixth and Major Seventh.**

>These three simply ask for the Harmonic Form with the Raised Seventh only. If you count the value of the interval from the First to the Raised Seventh, you will find it is a Major Seventh; while if you count from the first up to the sixth when it has not been raised, you will find it is a Minor Sixth.

(d) Write a Minor Scale ascending, **using a Major Sixth and a Major Seventh.**

(e) Write a Minor Scale, **using the Major Sixth and Seventh in ascending, and the Minor Seventh and Sixth in descending.**

>Both these questions simply ask for what has been called here the Melodic or Altered Diatonic Form. If you count the value of the interval from the first to the **Raised Sixth and Raised Seventh** in ascending, you will find them to be **Major Sixth and Major Seventh** respectively; whereas, if you count these in the descending scale after the seventh and sixth have been lowered again, you will find both intervals to be Minor.

The name **Sharp Seventh** is sometimes applied to the interval from the first to the seventh of the Minor Scale when the seventh has been raised.

The use of this name is to be regretted, as a **sharp interval** is usually understood to mean the same as an Augmented Interval, while in the case under consideration, the seventh is simply a Major Seventh.

The term **Flat** sixth, or **Flat** seventh is sometimes applied to this Minor Sixth and Minor Seventh respectively, but the name is not good for a similar reason to that just pointed out.

The following rules will be found useful when writing Minor Scales :—

   (a) The Minor (or flat) sixth, and the Minor (or flat) seventh are always shown **without** Accidentals.

   (b) The Major or sharp sixth and the Major or sharp seventh are always shown **with** Accidentals that raise, except in the case of the Tonic Minor.

137a. How to tell the Minor Key from the Signature. We will try and find out this by taking an example. Beginning with a Major Scale, say scale of G, signature F♯ the Relative Minor Scale is E Minor (G_1, A_2, B_3, C_4, D_5, E_6). Or descending a third, thus, G_1, F_2, E_3 in either case we find the Relative Minor key is E Minor, and the only sharp in the signature is F; then so far as this scale is concerned it would be correct to say that **the next note below the last sharp is the first of the Minor Scale,** just as it was pointed out in Art. 101, that **the next note above the last sharp is the first of the Major Scale.**

Let us try another example, and see if the same rule will hold. Begin with Major Scale of D, signature two sharps, F and C, the Relative Minor is B Minor (D_1, E_2, F_3, G_4, A_5, B_6). Or descending a third, thus, D_1, C_2, B_3 ; in either case we find the key is B Minor, and the last sharp is C ; but B is the next note below C, so again we find that **the next note below the last sharp is the first of the**

Minor Scale. This rule may now be committed to memory; if we try it in any other case we shall find it to be true also.

But if there be flats in the signature, what then? We shall see by an example. Beginning with B♭ Major, signature two flats, B and E, counting a sixth upwards, thus, B_1, C_2, D_3, E_4, F_5, G_6; or a third downwards, thus, B_1, A_2, G_3, we find the Relative Minor is G Minor.

Here then, the last flat in the signature is E, and the Minor Key is G, and G is a third above E; that is, **the key note, or first of the Minor Scale, is a third above the last flat**, just as it was pointed out in Art. 105 that the **key note, or first of the Major Scale, is a fourth below the last flat.**

Let us try another example to see if this rule will hold. Beginning with A♭ Major, signature four flats, B, E, A, D; counting a sixth upwards, thus, A_1, B_2, C_3, D_4, E_5, F_6; or a third downwards, thus, A_1, G_2, F_3, we find the Relative Minor is F Minor.

Here the key is F Minor, the last flat is D, and F is a third above D, so that again it is true to say that **the key note, or first of the Minor Scale, is a third above the last flat.** This rule may now be committed to memory; if applied in any other case you will find it to be true.

138. How to answer such questions as the following:— **What is the Relative Minor to B Major,** and what is its signature?

Count from B up to the sixth above it, thus: B_1, C_2, D_3, E_4, F_5, G_6, or count from B to the third below it, thus, B_1, A_2, G_3. Consider whether this G in the scale of B is **sharp, flat** or **natural.** It is **sharp**, then G♯ Minor is the Relative to B Major. What is its signature? The same as that of B Major, viz., five sharps, F, C, G, D and A.

What **quality** of Sixth is it from B up to G♯? A Major Sixth. Then how much may you say the key note of a Minor Scale is above the key note of its Relative Major Scale? A Major Sixth. How much is the key note of the Minor Scale below that of its Relative Major? **A Minor Third.**

Then how much may you say the key note of any Major Scale is **below** the key note of its Relative Minor? A Major Sixth. How much may you say the key note of any Major Scale is above that of its Relative Minor? **A Minor Third.** Then answer this question:—

What is the Relative Major to C Minor?

Count **down** to a sixth **below** C; C₁, B₂, A₃, G₄, F₅, E₆, or count **up** to the third **above** C; C₁, D₂, E₃.

In order that E may be a Major Sixth below C, or a **Minor Third** above C, whether is it to be **sharp, flat** or **natural?** It must be **flat**.

Then E♭ Major is the Relative to C Minor.

Give yourself plenty of exercises of this kind till you can answer with rapidity.

139. From what you have just learned you will now understand that any key signature may be the signature of two different scales, that is, it may be the signature of a Major Scale, or of the Relative Minor to that Major.

In the following table of key signatures the upper note shows the tonic of the Major Key corresponding to the signature and the lower note the tonic of its Relative Minor:—

You should practise yourself well in the foregoing manner upon all the key signatures, till you can tell with great rapidity the Major and Minor Scale of which each is the signature.

140. Sharps, Flats, Naturals, Double Flats or Double Sharps, used in a piece of music to alter notes (whether by raising or lowering them) otherwise than as shown by the key signature, are called **Accidentals**, that is, **Accidental** flats or sharps, &c. You have seen examples of them in every Minor Scale, but they are frequently used otherwise than in Minor Scales.

141. It may well be asked now, how can one tell whether the key is Major or Minor, since the same signature may indicate either the one or the other?

There are three ways of telling, viz. :—

(a) The last note in the Bass part is **usually** the key note of the scale. But as it is not **universally** so, this test is not always a reliable one.

(b) If the scale be Minor, on looking over the piece you will very soon notice the Accidentals, indicating the raised seventh of the Harmonic Form, or the raised sixth and seventh of the Melodic Form, and this may be taken as conclusive that the scale is Minor.

But both these tests apply to music **as written on the paper**, not as sung or played on an instrument.

(c) The **effect** of the Minor is very different from that of the Major.

The Minor is **plaintive** or **melancholy** in its character and effect, while the Major is **bold, grand, cheerful** in its character and effect; and this difference is so marked that there can be no mistaking it after a person has once realised it. But it is no use trying to describe it to you on paper; the thing is impossible; to appreciate it, you must, in the first instance, **hear** a piece of music in a Minor Key, and one in a Major Key, contrast the effects yourself, and no further demonstration will be needed.

When a piece of music is in a Major Key, it is said to be in the **Major Mode,** but when in a Minor Key it is said to be in the **Minor Mode.**

142. There is yet one more kind of Minor Scale which must now be mentioned. Before doing so it is necessary to introduce just one definition more.

The first note of any scale is called the **Tonic, or key note.**

Now, a Minor Scale with the same **Tonic** as any Major Scale is called the **Tonic Minor,** and the Major Scale with the same Tonic as any Minor Scale would be called the **Tonic Major.**

Some hold that the **Tonic Minor** is the proper **relative** to the **Tonic Major,** although they do not themselves call it by the name, Relative Minor.

Without entering upon a discussion of the conflicting views on this matter, the form of a **Tonic Minor** Scale is shown by the following example :—

Take any Major Scale as the scale of C. You are  already aware that the interval from the first to the third of this scale is a **Major Third.**

You are also aware (see Art. 127) that the interval from the first to the third of a Minor Scale is a **Minor Third,** so in order to produce this Minor Interval the third note of this scale is lowered, or depressed, and so is the sixth in order to produce a Minor Sixth. Hence we get the following as the ascending half of the **Tonic Minor** of C Major, the descending half being the same as the ascending :—

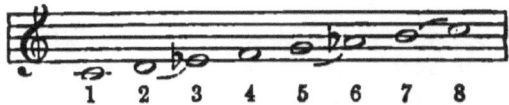

This is very like the Harmonic or Chromatic Form given in Art. 133, as it has the semitones between the **second** and **third,** the **fifth** and **sixth,** and **seventh** and **eighth** notes. Those who favour this call it the **Harmonic Minor Scale.**

But it has the defect pointed out in Art. 134, for there is an Augmented Second between the sixth and seventh notes.

Hence it is altered, if not in the same way, at any rate to produce the same effect, as in Art. 134.

The ascending and descending scales are different, the sixth is not depressed in the ascending scale, but both the seventh and sixth are depressed in the descending scale, and thus the Augmented Second is avoided in both.

This is called the Melodic Form of Tonic Minor.

You should write several Minor Scales after this pattern; there is nothing like **doing the thing yourself** in order to acquire a thorough knowledge of it; mere **telling**, or even **showing** by examples, is not enough.

Respecting the difference in signature between any Major Scale and its Tonic Minor, Melodic Form, you will find, no matter how many you write, that as in the example just written, **the Tonic Minor will have three flats more than the Tonic Major**, or when the signature consists of sharps **the Tonic Minor will have three sharps less than the Tonic Major**.

In the case of the signature F♯, as there are not three sharps to lose, the one sharp is lost and two flats are found necessary in the Tonic Minor; and in the case of the signature F♯ and C♯ again there are not three to lose, but the two are lost and one flat is found necessary.

It is to be observed that though these three extra flats are spoken of as belonging to the signature of the Minor Key, they are not written at the beginning of the piece with the usual key signature but introduced as Accidentals when required.

The following shows the **Intervals found in the Minor Scale** (ascending) Melodic Form. **Scale of E Minor** is taken as an example.

Seconds.—The second and seventh bear Minor Seconds; all the other degrees of the scale bear Major Seconds, except the sixth, which in the Harmonic or Chromatic Form bears an Augmented Second.

Thirds.—The first, second, sixth and seventh bear Minor Thirds; all the other degrees of the scale bear Major Thirds.

Fourths.—The third and fourth bear Tritone or Augmented Fourths, indicated by ∧; the seventh bears a **Diminished** Fourth, indicated by ∨; all the others bear Perfect Fourths.

Fifths.—The sixth and seventh bear Diminished Fifths indicated by ∨; the third bears an Augmented Fifth; all the others bear Perfect Fifths.

Sixths.—The first, second, third, and fourth bear Major Sixths; the fifth, sixth, and seventh, bear Minor Sixths.

Sevenths.—The first and third bear Major Sevenths; the second, fourth, fifth and sixth, bear Minor Sevenths; the seventh bears a Diminished Seventh.

In any other Minor Scale in the form given above, the first, second, third, &c., degrees of the scale will bear intervals of exactly the same kind and **quality** as those found in the Scale of E Minor. Try it, by writing other scales and forming intervals from seconds to sevenths on each note.

Write all the other forms of the Minor Scale; form intervals similarly on each note, and mark carefully any differences you may discover in the **quality** of intervals of the same kind, and on same degrees of the scale as in the exercise given above.

Observe that the following intervals found in the Minor Scale, are not found in any Major Diatonic Scale, viz.:— Augmented Second; Augmented Fifth; Diminished Seventh; Diminished Fourth. Refer to list of Intervals at the end of Art. 125.

The Augmented Second is found between the lower (or flat) sixth and the Leading Note; the Augmented Fifth between the third note of the scale and the Leading Note; the Diminished Seventh and the Diminished Fourth are the inversions of the Augmented Second and Fifth, respectively, and are both found on the Leading Note. Thus in the key of C Minor we have:—

You should make yourself well acquainted with the particular forms of Minor Scale in which these occur: they have all been pointed out in the preceding Articles.

142a. Naming the Key.—The study of Minor keys which we have just completed makes it clear that it is now necessary to add something to what was said on this point in Arts. 101*a*, 105*a*, 187*a*, and 139. Questions on naming the key may come before you in several different forms, such as:—

First.—When all the sharps or flats necessary for determining the key are present and written *as a key signature* at the beginning of the piece. Cases of this kind have been so fully dealt with in the Articles named above, and to which the student is again referred, that it is unnecessary to say anything further on the point here.

Second.—When all the sharps or flats necessary for determining the key are present, *not written as a key signature*, but scattered over the piece. All that you have to do is to go over the piece carefully, take each sharp or flat as you meet it, and write it in its position in a signature; then on seeing all the sharps or all the flats together determine the key as previously explained. If the same sharp or flat occurs more than once in the piece, as will often be the case, do not write it more than once in the signature.

Example 1:—

Here though there are three sharps written in the piece, it is clear there are only two *different* ones, F and C, so by Art. 101*a* we see at once the key is D Major, as there is nothing to suggest any other.

Example 2:—

Here neglecting the flats repeated, and putting the others in proper order, we find the four flats, B, E, A, D, so we see at once by Art. 105*a* the key is A flat Major, as there is nothing to suggest any other.

Example 3 :—

Here on rejecting the repeated sharps we still find three different ones remaining, viz., F, C, and A, but these do not form any signature in the Table in Art. 101, since before A can occur in any signature we must have G and D before it as well as F and C ; so we must look for some explana‧tion. The two sharps, F and C, come correctly in order ; they may indicate the key of D Major, or its relative, B Minor. If they indicate D Major, then A♯ would not be required, but if they denote B Minor, then A♯ would be correctly used as the raised seventh of the Minor scale. Hence we conclude the key is B Minor, and we are further confirmed in this belief by observing that the piece ends with the tonic B.

Third.—When some of the sharps or flats necessary for determining the key are written as a key signature at the beginning of the piece, and the others are added throughout the piece. This can only occur when there is a modulation (see Arts. 145 to 153), or when the key is Minor. In this latter case the signature written at the beginning will be found to be the ordinary signature of a Major key, and of its relative Minor ; the accidentals then used throughout the piece will be found to denote the raised seventh, and perhaps the raised sixth also, of the Minor key.

Example 4 :—

Here the sharps, F, C, G, D, in the signature may indicate the key of E Major, but they may also indicate the relative Minor of E, that is C♯ Minor ; and on observing the accidentals used throughout the piece, we observe that A♯ and B♯ are both used, and as these are the sixth and seventh of the scale of C♯ Minor, we conclude that these accidentals indicate the raised sixth and seventh, hence we conclude the key is C♯ Minor.

Example 5:—

Here the B♭ in the signature may indicate the key of F Major, or its relative Minor, D Minor; we conclude it is D Minor because we see at once the C♯ introduced indicates the raised seventh of the Minor key; hence the key is D Minor.

Fourth.—When only some of the sharps or flats necessary for determining the key signature are present, and they are not written as a signature, but scattered over the piece of music as in the following examples.

Example 6:—

On examining this we find three different sharps, F, C and D; but we never find F, C, and D written as a key signature; we must always have G before we can have D. On looking along the G line for G♯ we find the note G does not occur in the piece at all, so that there was no opportunity of showing G♯: hence we conclude that G♯ is understood, that the signature is four sharps, F, C, G and D, and that it indicates the key of E Major. Observe that though F and C alone might indicate D Major, or its relative Minor, B Minor, still the additional sharp D is not the one that would be required to indicate either the raised sixth, or the raised seventh of that key.

Example 7:—

On examining this we find three different sharps, F, C and A; but these three never occur as a sharp signature of a Major key; before we can have A♯ in any signature we must have not only F and C, but also G and D Sharp. The note G does not occur in the passage, but D does occur in it, and D is not sharp, so we cannot conclude, as in the last example, that G♯ and D♯ are understood. We take F♯ and C♯ as being the proper signature, indicating not the Major key of D, but its relative Minor B, and then A♯ is correctly used, indicating the raised seventh of the Minor key. Hence the key is B Minor.

Example 8 :—

On examining this we find three different flats, B, A, and D, but these three never form a key signature; before we can have either A♭ or D♭, we must have E♭ in the signature. On further examining the piece to see if we may conclude that E♭ is understood, we find that impossible, for E is expressed, and E is natural. Now it is true a natural is not required before E under the circumstances to indicate that it is natural, yet if there were a ♮ there, it would suggest what is the solution of the whole difficulty. The signature is four flats, B, E, A, and D; it indicates not A♭ Major, but F Minor which contains E♭; the E♮ is then the raised seventh of the Minor key.

Fifth.—When the key signature is written in the usual way at the beginning of the piece, but is immediately contradicted either wholly or partially by accidentals occurring throughout the piece.

Example 9 :—

Here the signature is three flats, B, E, and A, which would seem to indicate the key of E♭ major, but on looking over the piece we find B♮ contradicting the B♭ in the signature; also E♮ and A♮ contradicting the E♭ and A♭ in the signature; so that we now find the same circumstances as if there were no signature at all: hence we conclude the key is C major.

Example 10 :—

Here we have not only the same contradiction of signature as in Example 9, but we have additional accidentals, viz., F♯, C♯, and G♯, forming in themselves a new signature, and indicating the key of A major.

Example 11 :—

Here we have as signature two sharps, F and C, apparently indicating the key of D major, but on looking over the piece we find the C♯ at once contradicted by the C♮ in the first bar while F♯ remains throughout the piece. We also find B♭ and E♭ introduced, these would of themselves constitute a new correct signature, but we have then to account for the presence of F♯. The two flats indicate the key of B♭ major, or its relative minor, G minor; taking them to indicate the latter, we see at once that F♯ is the raised seventh of the minor scale, hence we conclude definitely the key is G minor.

Many more examples might be given, but I think I have given sufficient to enable the student to see the nature of the thoughts that must pass through his mind before he can answer questions of this class, and unless he will take the trouble to think as suggested no number of additional examples will enable him to answer correctly.

CHAPTER VI.

Mental Effects. — Modulation.

Transposition.—Relative Keys.

143. In Art. 142 you learned that the **First** note of a scale is called the **Tonic,** or **Key Note**; you also learned in Art. 182 that the **Seventh** note of any scale is called the **Leading Note,** and you learned why it is so-called. To each of the other notes in the scale a special name is also given.

The **Fifth** is called the **Dominant.** It is so called on account of its great importance, being, next to the Tonic, the most important note in the scale, but as this to a great extent depends upon the nature of the chord founded on it, the full measure of its importance cannot be explained till you enter upon the study of Harmony.

The **Fourth** is called the **Sub-dominant** because it is the fifth note **below** the Tonic, just as the true Dominant is the fifth note **above** the tonic.

The **Third** is called the **Mediant,** because it is **midway** between Tonic and Dominant.

The **Sixth** is called the **Sub-mediant** because, proceeding *downwards*, it comes midway between the Tonic and **Sub**-dominant.

The **Second** is called the **Super-tonic** because it is next immediately *above* the tonic.

Each note of the scale also produces its own peculiar mental effect on the hearer, and students should, as early as possible, make themselves acquainted with those effects; once they are realised a great part of the difficulty in the art of singing will be overcome,

The effects are produced chiefly by relation and contrast and while it is impossible to realise the mental effects without hearing the notes in some sort of succession, the following statement of the effects will stimulate the observation whenever there is an opportunity of hearing the notes sung slowly:—

Tonic	Strength, firmness.
Super-tonic ...	Hopefulness.
Mediant ...	Calmness, steadiness.
Sub-dominant	Desolation, awe.
Dominant ...	Grandeur, brightness.
Sub-mediant...	Sadness, weeping.
Leading Note	Sensitiveness, expectancy, desire.

The artist in composing his music takes advantage of these natural characteristics of the notes to produce the effect he desires; thus the frequent recurrence of a note with a particular effect, especially if it recur at the important parts, that is, at the accented parts of the bars, cannot fail to impress that general effect upon a whole passage.

144. While it nearly always happens that any musical composition, no matter how long, ends in the same key with which it began, it hardly ever happens that any composition, no matter how short, continues in the same key throughout.

There is change from one key to another for the sake of variety.

This change from one key to another is called **Modulation**. It is also called **Transition**.

The question then naturally arises, may Modulation take place from any one key whatever into any other key whatever? The answer is decidedly, No. Why so? Because, if, for instance, a piece begins in the Common Scale, and after a time there is Modulation into a new key with three or four sharps in the signature, or with four or five flats in the signature, the introduction of so many new notes produces such a violent change that, unless under very exceptional circumstances, the effect is displeasing to the ear rather than otherwise. A great artist may produce great effects by unusual transition, but the beginner must carefully adhere to the following law.

145. What, then, is the law which governs Modulation ?

In Art. 97 you learned what is the **Natural Order of Scale Formation,** and you there saw that the order is to proceed from one scale to another, **differing from it in one note only**; you saw that while the signature consists of **sharps** this is effected by ascending a (Perfect) **Fifth** for the Tonic of each new scale, viz., from C to G ; from G to D ; from D to A ; from A to E ; and so on.

You also saw that while the signature consists of **flats** this is effected by ascending a (Perfect) **Fourth** for the Tonic of each new scale, viz., from C to F ; from F to B♭ ; from B♭ to E♭ ; and so on.

This gives us the principle underlying the Law of Modulation in the majority of cases.

146. Modulation generally takes place from one key into another containing only one new note, that is, from any key into another key containing **one sharp more, or one sharp less,** in the signature; or, **one flat more, or one flat less,** in the signature; or there may be Modulation from any Major Key to its relative Minor, or from any Minor Key to its relative Major.

147. The key in which any composition begins is called the **Principal Key** of the piece, or sometimes the **Original Key.**

The key into which Modulation takes place is called the **Subordinate Key or Secondary Key.**

There may be Modulation from one Subordinate Key to another, under the same conditions as from the Principal to a Subordinate Key, so that there may be, and there will be, several Subordinate Keys in a composition of any considerable length.

148. From Art 145, then, it appears that Modulation should be from the Principal Key (or a Subordinate Key) into a key **a Perfect Fifth higher,** or **a Perfect Fifth lower,** or **a Perfect Fourth higher,** or a **Perfect**

Fourth lower, as, for instance, from the Key of D, with two sharps in the signature, to that of A, a fifth above D, with three sharps in the signature; or to that of G, a fifth below D, with one sharp in signature; or, as another example, from the Key of B♭, with two flats in the signature, to that of E♭, a Perfect Fourth above B♭, with three flats in the signature; or to that of F, a Perfect Fourth below B♭, with one flat in the signature. The following is an example :—

In the fifth bar of this example the G♯ shows that modulation has taken place into the Key of A, whose Tonic is a **Perfect Fifth higher** than that of D, the Principal Key, and the recurrence of G♯ in the seventh bar shows that the piece continues in the Key of A.

Again, in the following example :—

The presence of A♭ in the third bar indicates modulation into the Key of E♭, whose Tonic is a **Perfect Fifth below** that of B♭, the Principal Key, and the recurrence of the A♭ in the fourth bar shows that the piece continues in the Key of E♭.

149. If there be any given key, then the key a Perfect Fifth above it, the key a Perfect Fifth below it, the key a Perfect Fourth above it, and the key a Perfect Fourth below it are called **Relatives** of the given key. They are also called **Attendant** Keys.

It is worth your attention to note that though four Relative Keys seem to be mentioned here, there are in reality only two mentioned, for a Perfect Fifth **above** and a Perfect Fourth **below** any given note are one and the same, as you will easily see if you take the trouble to count. Also a Perfect Fourth **above** and a Perfect Fifth **below** any given note are one and the same.

150. Hence you see that any Major Key has two Relative or Attendant Keys, **also Major**, and as each of these three (that is the Principal Key and two Major Relatives), has a Relative Minor, there are altogether **six Relative keys**, three Major, and three Minor, viz.:

The Principal Key (Major).

The key **a** Perfect Fifth **above** the Principal (Major).

The key **a** Perfect Fifth **below** the Principal (Major), and

The Relative Minors of these three Majors.

It is just the same with a Minor Key (as the Principal Key may be either Major or Minor); its Relatives are:—

The Minor Key a Perfect Fifth above the Principal.

The Minor Key a Perfect Fifth below the Principal, and

The **Relative Majors** of the three Minors.

This, then, completes what is but partially stated in Arts. 144 and 145. **Modulation** should, as a rule, take place from any one key into one of the five Relative or Attendant Keys.

151. When Modulation takes place from any key to one of its Relatives it is termed **Natural Modulation**, but when into a **remote** or **distant** key it is termed **Extraneous Modulation**.

One key is said to be **remote** or **distant** from another when their signatures differ by more than one sharp or flat, and of course some keys are more remote than others from any given key.

152. How is this Modulation indicated on paper? Suppose a composer is writing in the Key of D, he has two sharps, F and C, written at the beginning of his composition, as the signature. He now wishes to **modulate** into the scale of A with three sharps in the signature, F, C and G; does he stop and write this new signature in full? No; he merely inserts, **as an Accidental**, a ♯ before the note G when it occurs, and that Accidental along with the signature at the beginning sufficiently indicates that he is now in the Key of A. (See example Art. 148.)

Or again; suppose, writing in the Scale of D, he wants to modulate into the Scale of G, he simply inserts, **as an Accidental**, a ♮ before the note C when it occurs. This ♮ contradicts the ♯ in the signature at the beginning, which now becomes one ♯ only, thus indicating the Key of G as required.

When he wishes to return to the Key of D he writes as an **Accidental** a ♯ before C when it occurs, thus restoring the original signature and indicating the Key of D.

These modulations are seen in the following example:—

And similarly in any other case. If a ♭ is to be added to the signature to indicate a change of key, only that one ♭ is written, and it is inserted **as an Accidental** where required.

If the ♭ is to be taken away from the signature at the beginning, the insertion of a ♮ when and where required sufficiently indicates this.

In the case of **Extraneous Modulation** the new key signature is frequently written, as a whole, after a Double Bar. This will always be the case when, as often happens, a new time signature is introduced simultaneously with the new key signature.

153. Then do all Accidentals indicate Modulation? No. How, then, can we tell what ones do and what ones do not indicate Modulation? Very easily if we know the key signatures properly as given in Arts. 101, 105, and 139.

If we know the order in which **sharps** or **flats** invariably occur in signatures, we can have no difficulty in telling in any case whether a given **flat** or **sharp** would be a **proper** addition to the signature, or whether a given **natural** indicates what would be a **proper** removal of a **flat** or **sharp** from a signature.

To make that clear by example: Suppose the signature of the Principal Key is two sharps, F and C, and a little way on you find a ♯ introduced before A, you are to think thus—Is A the next sharp that comes in a signature after F and C? No. What would be next? G. And what next? D. All before A? Yes. Then what conclusion do you draw? That this ♯ before A does not indicate Modulation.

Very good, so far, but don't be too hasty with conclusions. You are right in concluding that the A♯ does not indicate Modulation into a Relative Major Key.

But that does not exhaust the subject for your consideration. There are Relative **Minor** Keys, you know. Yes, you say, but they have the **same** signature as the Major.

That is true; but you know you learned in Art. 183 that there is such a thing as a **raised seventh** in the Minor Scale, and occasionally a **raised sixth** also, and that these are always indicated by Accidentals.

Yes, you say, but must we think of all that over here? Indeed we must, and a beautiful thought it is at the present moment: let us dwell upon it.

The given signature is two sharps, F and C.

What is the Major Key indicated? Key of D.

What is the Relative Minor to D? B Minor.

And what is the seventh note of B Minor? A, of course, Now, what do you think of the Accidental ♯ before A? It may indicate the **raised seventh** of B Minor. Very good, it **may** indicate it, but it **does not necessarily** do so; if you see it again very soon, and in particular if you see the raised sixth (G♯) along with it you may conclude for a certainty that there is Modulation into B minor.

Proceed similarly in any other case, never forgetting either the Accidentals required for the Relative Minor, or those required for the Tonic Minor, and you can have no difficulty in deciding whether any given Accidental indicates Modulation or not.

In Art. 92 you saw that the black keys on an instrument may be called by two different names, for instance, one may be either C♯ or D♭, another may be D♯ or E♭, and so on.

If we have any note such as C♯, and we substitute D♭ for it, thus **changing** the **name** of the note **without altering** its **pitch**, this change is called **Enharmonic** alteration.

If there be an Enharmonic alteration of note which produces a change of key, then this change is called **Enharmonic Modulation,** but the subject is too advanced to be dealt with in this elementary book.

Besides the meaning given to **Modulation** in the previous articles, it also means in music, as in reading, the adaptation of the tone of voice to the sentiment to be expressed.

154. You learned in Art. 88 that each note in a scale bears a certain known fixed relation to the Tonic and to each of the other notes in the scale.

Hence we have been able to form several scales to one pattern by maintaining this relation.

In like manner, if there be a piece of music in any key whatever, and beginning on a certain note in that key, we may begin the same piece on a note higher or lower than the given one, by a known interval, and if we make each note throughout the piece higher or lower than the given notes by the same interval (that is preserving the same relation between the new notes that existed between the given ones), we are said to change the piece into **a new key,** higher or lower as the case may be, and the **tune** will remain the same as at first.

155. The **act of writing** out or performing any given piece of music in a key higher or lower than the given one is called **Transposition.**

It is not a difficult operation for any one who has mastered the chapters on Intervals and Scales. The method of doing it is best seen from an example.

Transpose the following into a new key, a Major Second higher:—

The given piece, as you see from the signature, is in the key of G Major. We are asked to transpose it into a new key, a Major Second higher. What note is a Major Second higher than G? A is. Then we are asked to transpose the given piece into the scale of A Major. So all we have to do is to set down the signature of A Major on the staff, and then write for each of the given notes a note a Major Second higher. Thus, instead of G write A; instead of A write B; instead of B write C♯, and observe that an Accidental **will not be necessary** to indicate the C♯, as C is sharp by the signature, that of A Major being three sharps, F, C and G, and so on throughout the piece, no matter how long.

But as you learned in Arts. 108 to 115 that **whatever** interval exists between the first and second, first and third, first and fourth, &c., notes of any Major Scale, the **same** interval exists between the first and second, first and third, first and fourth, &c., notes of **any other** Major Scale, the following will be found the simplest plan in transposition:—

Write down the given piece, and under each note set down its number with reference to the Tonic, that is, set down the figure which indicates whether the note is the first, second, third, fourth, fifth, sixth, seventh, or eighth of the scale.

Now set down the signature of the new scale on a staff, and set down the same degrees, **numerically,** of the new scale that you found given of the old scale.

It is important to remember that the new key signature must never be omitted when transposing.

156. Should an Accidental occur in the given piece, all you have to do is to introduce an Accidental **producing the same effect** in the transposed piece.

Observe that this does not mean that if there be an Accidental **sharp** in the given piece, you must therefore have an Accidental **sharp** in the transposed piece.

An Accidental **sharp** indicates the **raising** of a note by a semitone. Now, suppose that the signature of your transposed piece consists of **flats,** and that it is one of the notes **flat** by signature that must be raised a semitone, then the raising is done by inserting a ♮ to contradict the ♭ in the signature; so that a ♮ in the transposed piece may **produce the same effect** as a ♯ in the given piece.

In like manner a ♭ in the transposed piece may **produce the same effect** as a ♮ in the given piece; or a ♯ in the transposed piece may **produce the same effect** as a ♮ in the given piece, if the signature in the latter consists of flats, and the ♮ is a contradiction of one of them, indicating the accidental raising of a note.

What has been said on Transposition relates to either Major or Minor Keys, but it is to be understood that there can be no change of **Mode** by the Transposition. If the given piece were in a Major Key, it remains in a Major Key after Transposition, whereas if the given piece were in a Minor Key, it remains in a Minor Key after Transposition.

157. If the Accidental in the given piece indicates Modulation, then the one which you use to **produce the same effect** will undoubtedly indicate Modulation also, whether you advert to the fact or not.

The following is an example of transposition of a piece in which no Modulation takes place.

Transpose the following a Minor Third lower.

Here the Tonic is B♭; count and set down the number of each note with reference to the Tonic, as you see done above.

ɪ

Then think what will the new scale be; it is to be a Minor Third lower than B♭, that will be G: the new key is G; signature one sharp, viz., F. Write down a staff, put one sharp on it in its proper place, and then where you find 1, 3, 2 . . . . 7, 6, 5, &c., of the original scale as given above set down the 1, 3, 2 . . . . 7, 6, 5, &c., of the new scale, thus:—

The following is an example of transposition of a piece in which Modulation takes place.

Transpose the following a Major Third higher:—

Here the given key is A♭; a Major Third higher than A♭ is C **natural**; so you are asked to transpose this into the scale of C. Proceed exactly as directed in the last example.

The only additional point to be noticed is, that in the first bar before the note D there is an Accidental; it is placed before a note, **flat according to signature**. The ♮ then indicates the note is to be raised a semitone; you are to use an Accidental that will **produce the same effect**, that is, one that will raise the corresponding note in the transposed piece a semitone. As this note is **natural** in the transposed piece you are ʳ use a ♯ to raise it a semitone.

Hence you get the following transposition. No key signature is required, as it is the Key of C.

What does this F♯ in the first bar of the transposed piece indicate? Clearly it indicates Modulation from the Key of C into that of G, that is, into a key a Fifth higher in the **natural order of Scale Formation**.

What did the D♮ indicate in the piece to be transposed? Clearly it indicated Modulation from A♭ into E♭, that is a **Fifth higher**, but in this case it is better to say a Fourth lower. (See Art. 149.)

So you see that if an Accidental, whether it be ♯, ♭ or ♮, indicates Modulation in the piece to be transposed, the Accidental which **produces the same effect** in the transposed piece will also indicate Modulation.

Transpose the following a Minor Third lower, namely, into the Key of E Minor.

The above passage is in G Minor, and, as was stated in a previous paragraph, it remains in a Minor Key after transposition.

The key being G Minor, the tonic is G, and not B♭. The new key being E Minor, the signature will be one sharp, viz., F.

The following shows the transposition: The Accidentals inserted do not show Modulation; they are only the raised

Seventh, and the raised Sixth respectively of the Minor Scale.

After doing several exercises you will become so expert that the figures will be a hindrance rather than a help, and you will dispense with them altogether.

157a. In writing new scales, or in modulating from one scale or key to another, some musicians call the first note of the new scale by the syllabic name, **Do**, no matter what the scale may be, and call the other notes of the scale in succession by the syllabic names, Re, Mi, Fa, Soh, La, Ti, Do. This is called the **Movable Do System**, because instead of *Do* being fixed to the middle C line as we have so far considered it (and thus have been unconsciously using the **Fixed Do System**), it moves in the scale of G to the second line, or in the scale of B to the third line, and so on. Thus the series of notes in the second of the following examples would be called by the same syllabic names as the first.

Example 12 :—

Do Re Mi Fa Sol La Ti Do   Do Re Mi Fa Sol La Ti Do

Similarly each of the series of notes given in all the scales in Arts. 98 and 108 would be called by the syllabic names, Do, Re, Mi, Fa, Sol, La, Ti, Do. There is some advantage in this, because the relations of the notes, Do, Re, &c., to one another having been once properly learned in the scale of C, or Common scale, it is easy to preserve that relation when the tonic is taken at any pitch different from C; and this advantage is intensified by slightly modifying the names of the notes to signify that they are flat or sharp, as for instance calling Fa sharp *Fee*; La sharp, *Lee*; or calling Mi flat, *Maw*; Ti flat, *Taw*; and so on.

Against this advantage, which is very great practically, must be placed the disadvantage that lies in the difficulty of naming the notes, if we no longer associate the name of a particular note with a particular line or a particular space on the staff. This disadvantage does not equal the advantage just pointed out, and even this disadvantage may be overcome by remembering that if the tonic or key note be on a line, then the third, fifth, and seventh of the scale will each be on a line also, while the second, fourth, sixth, and octave will each be on a space, as in the following examples:—

Example 13:—

Similarly, if we move the **Do** up to the second line, that is, give it the pitch of G, the new **Do** being on a line, the new **Mi, Sol, Ti** will also be on lines; while the **Re, Fa, La,** and upper **Do** will be on spaces, thus:—

Example 14:—

Similarly, if the new **Do** be in a space, then **Mi, Sol, Ti,** will also be in spaces; and **Re, Fa, La, Do** will be on lines as in the following example, in which the new **Do** is placed in the first space, thus giving it the pitch of F:—

Example 15:—

A little practice will make the student familiar with the position each note should occupy in relation to any position of the key note, or **Do**, as the key note is always called in this system. When this system is adopted, transposition can never be looked upon as a difficult operation ; it is merely a change of pitch to higher or lower, and once the position of the new key note is found there can be no further difficulty.

Note that, as stated in Art. 10, **Re** is to be pronounced **Ray**.

The present affords a favourable opportunity for adding something about Intervals, which it was not thought convenient to state in the chapter dealing with Intervals. Nothing was there said about Intervals beyond the Octave, but, as you have seen several of these in the example just finished, it may be as well now to say something about them.

In some of the examples lately written, if we reckon all the Intervals from middle C, you will find ninths, tenths, elevenths, twelfths.

When you come to study Harmony, you will have to recognise such Intervals as ninths, elevenths and thirteenths ; but at present we shall not use these names for Intervals larger than the Octave.

Intervals larger than the Octave may be called **Compound Intervals.**

For example: from middle C to D on the fourth line is a ninth ; we shall call it a **Compound Second**: from middle C to E in fourth space, we shall call, not a tenth, but a **Compound Third**, and so on.

The word **Compound**, however, is not very generally used, and it is quite usual to speak of the Interval from C to E simply as a third, even if C be in the **Great Octave** and E **In Altissimo**.

158. A piece of music may also be changed from one kind of **Time** to another.

Transcription is the name usually applied to the act of writing on paper the conversion of a piece of music from one kind of **Time** to another.

You will have noticed in studying the chapter on **Time** that the Time Notes (𝅝, 𝅗𝅥, 𝅘𝅥, 𝅘𝅥𝅮, &c.) used in a piece of music, give but a very imperfect intimation of what the **pace** or rate of movement is to be. What is expressed by these notes is merely a **relation** of time, and as there is the same relation between a 𝅗𝅥 and a 𝅘𝅥 that there is between a 𝅘𝅥 and a 𝅘𝅥𝅮, it is clear that if we change every 𝅗𝅥 in a piece into a 𝅘𝅥, and every 𝅘𝅥 into a 𝅘𝅥𝅮, and if we do the same, that is to **halve** every note, throughout a whole piece, the same relation as before will still exist between the lengths of the various notes. The following is an example :—

Transcribe the following from 3/2 into 3/4 Time.

As given, the time is 3/2, that is, three minims in a bar, we are asked to make it 3/4 time, that is three crotchets in a bar. All we have to do is to **halve** each note and rest.

The following shows this done :—

Observe the foregoing as an example of what is stated in Art. 50, viz., that when the first and last Bars are incomplete the two together make up a complete Bar.

The foregoing transcription need not necessarily indicate any change of pace at all. You saw in Art. 79 that **actual pace** is indicated by a sign placed at the beginning of the piece and having reference to the Metronome.

Suppose at the beginning of the piece, as written in 3/2 time, we find 𝅗𝅥 = M 80, indicating that 80 minims are to be played or sung in a minute of time, and if we now place at the beginning of the piece as transposed into 3/4 time the sign ♩ = M 60, indicating that 60 crotchets are to be played in a minute of time, there is no change whatever in the **pace**, since 30 minims equal 60 crotchets.

159. In like manner we may transcribe from one kind of Time to another by **doubling** the value of each note and rest. As an example transcribe the following from 2/4 into 2/2 Time :—

Observe that when doubling a note we do not write it twice over, but write one note equal to twice the value. Thus : ♩ doubled = 𝅗𝅥 and not ♩♩

The given signature is 2/4, meaning two crotchets to a bar. We are asked to transpose into 2/2 Time, meaning two minims to a bar. As a minim is **double** a crotchet all we have to do is to write the signature 2/2 and **double** each note given, thus :—

In any transcription from one Time to another—

(a) **The number of the given notes must not be altered.**

(b) **The number or position of the bar lines must not be altered.**

(c) **And, as a consequence of the two foregoing, the position of the accents will remain unaltered.**

160. The examples given are the most usual kinds of Transcriptions of Time, viz., when each of the given notes is to be either **halved** or **doubled.**

But sometimes you are required to transcribe from one Time to another, when each note is to be made 2/3 of the given one, or 3/2 of the given one.

The method of doing this is best seen from an example.

Transcribe the following from 9/8 into 3/4 Time:—

Here the given signature is 9/8, meaning **nine** quavers to the bar, or, as it is usually expressed, three **dotted** crotchets (= nine quavers) to the bar, and we are asked to transcribe into 3/4 time, meaning three crotchets in a bar. Now this would be very easy if the given notes had all been **dotted** crotchets. Simply to write **crotchets** instead of **dotted crotchets** is all that would have been required.

But to be able to perform the exercise, in no matter what form it may be presented, it is necessary to **consider the relation of the crotchet to the dotted crotchet.**

In Art. 46 you learned that the dotted crotchet is as long and a half as the crotchet, that is, the dotted crotchet is 3/2 of the crotchet.

Also a crotchet equals **two** quavers; a dotted crotchet equals **three** quavers, so that a crotchet is 2/3 of a dotted crotchet.

This gives us the key to what is to be done, **each of the given notes must be made 2/3 of what it now is,** since the whole bar is to be made 2/3 of what it was, viz., six quavers instead of nine.

This is very easily done in the case of the dotted crotchets and minims. Remove the dot and that is all that is required.

But in the first bar there is a little difficulty with the three quavers. The 2/3 of 3 is 2, but you have just learned that we must not alter the number of notes, so the difficulty is to reduce these three quavers to the time of two without reducing their number.

Put the Triplet sign ⌢₃ over them, and as you learned in Art. 82 that indicates that the three are to be played or sung in the time of two, and that is just what we wanted.

Hence we obtain the following transcription:—

Note carefully this use of the Triplet sign, and it will serve you on other occasions.

161. As another example.

Transcribe the following from ¾ into ⁶⁄₈ time:—

Here, the given signature is ²⁄₄, meaning two crotchets in a bar. We are asked to transcribe into ⁶⁄₈ time, meaning six quavers in a bar, which is equal to three crotchets, but as stated in Art. 68, ⁶⁄₈ time is usually spoken of as two **dotted crotchets** in a bar.

Instead of **two crotchets** in a bar, then, we want to have **two dotted crotchets,** that is, we want to have **as much and a half** in each bar as before. Hence, each note must be made as long and a half.

The general plan of doing this is, turn each **note** into a dotted note, that is, dot the minims and crotchets; but with the quavers there is a little difficulty, not that the quavers are anything more difficult in themselves, but in consequence of their being tied in triplets in this example.

In the first bar you have a triplet in a form in which you did not meet it before; you have a crotchet and a quaver tied, but that is equal to three quavers, and the mark ⌒₃ is used as usual to indicate that the three quavers are to be played or sung in the same time as two, just as in the second and fifth bars, where the three quavers are written in the usual fashion.

Now, suppose we remove the mark ⌒₃, then the three quavers will get the time of three, for there will be nothing to indicate otherwise, and as three is **as much and a half** as two, that is all that is required.

Hence we obtain the following transcription :—

As another example, re-write the following in ¼ time, preserving the relative values and accents.

If the above remarks have been understood, you will have no difficulty in seeing that the following is the solution :—

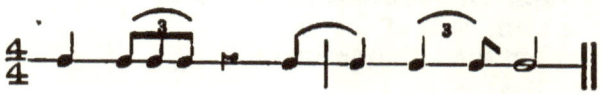

When these examples have been studied carefully, no difficulty will be found in any ordinary piece of transcription from one time to another.

CHAPTER VII.

Double Bars—Various Terms—Grace Notes—Terms Relating to Pace, Expression, and Style.

162. In the previous chapters only such terms were introduced as were thought necessary for a proper understanding of the various points dealt with.

Some other terms and marks will now be explained: they are frequently met with in music, in connection with the points already explained, and as they vary, modify, and in some instances nullify marks already explained, it is necessary to be acquainted with them.

The **Double Bar** consists of two lines drawn vertically across the staff, each of the lines being thicker than the ordinary Bar lines, thus:—

It marks the end of a composition, or an important portion of a composition, having some completeness in itself, somewhat as a sentence terminated by a full stop has completeness in itself, but yet is only a portion of a paragraph, which again is only a portion of something more extensive still.

Except at the end of a composition, the position of the Double Bar may or may not correspond with that of the ordinary Bar line, and as it has no reference to time, when its position does not correspond with that of the ordinary Bar line, the time is in no way affected, and as a consequence, neither is the accent.

163. Sometimes the Double Bar has dots before it, thus:—

The dots then indicate that the music is to be **repeated** from the beginning up to this point, or **from the previous Double Bar**, which would then have dots after it, thus:—

The initials **D.C.**, or the words **Da Capo**, are to be understood to mean, **repeat from the beginning** till you meet the word **Fine**, or a **Pause**, thus ⌢.

164. The **Pause** ⌢ is a contradiction not only of the relative time value of the note over which it is placed, but also of its actual **pace** value, as determined by reference to the Metronomic Signature at the beginning of the piece.

It signifies that the performer may dwell upon that note as long as he thinks fit.

It is frequently accompanied by the words **Ad Libitum**, usually **Ad Lib.**, signifying **at the performer's will or pleasure.** But **Ad Lib.** has often a more extended meaning given to it; it may refer to a whole **Passage**, and then the performer may alter the time of the passage at his will.

Even when applied to a single note only, **Ad Lib.** may have a more extended meaning, so that the performer may not only alter the time of the note but may **ornament** it as he pleases. For ornaments, see **Grace Notes**, 167.

165. Al Segno, or **Dal Segno,** meaning **to the sign,** is another mark used to indicate **repetition**, and means that the performer is to return to the sign 𝄋 at some previous portion of the piece, and repeat from that.

166. 8ve ⁓⁓⁓⁓⁓⁓⁓ written **over** a passage signifies that it is to be performed an octave higher than it is written.

8ve ⁓⁓⁓⁓⁓⁓⁓ written **under** a passage signifies that it is to be performed an octave lower than it is written.

This is a convenient method of avoiding a number of leger lines above or below the staff. When there is to be a return to the pitch at which the notes are actually written, the word **loco** is inserted thus:—8ve ⁓⁓⁓⁓ loco.

167. Grace Notes are small notes used along with principal notes for the purpose of ornament. They are in no way essential, and may be omitted without any other detriment to the music than the small points of beauty which it would lose thereby.

168. The Appoggiatura, of which an example is here given, is one of these; the small note E takes half the length from the note D, so  that, in reckoning the beats in the measure, E would not be counted at all.

In the case of a dotted note, the Appoggiatura takes one third of the length from it.

Observe that in the example given above, the D might be a quaver, the E might still be written as it is, and the meaning would remain just the same.

The **Leaning Note** is another name for the Appoggiatura.

169. The Acciaccatura, called also the **Crushing Note,** is another of these ornaments, of which two examples are given, showing that it may consist of either one or two small notes preceding the principal note. In either case the Acciaccatura is very brief, it does not take half or any definite portion from the principal note; it is merely to be touched momentarily; the performer must then pass on to the principal note, but whatever the duration may be, it is taken from that of the principal note.

When the Acciaccatura consists of a single note a semitone *below* the principal note, it is termed a Beat, as:—

Of course the word **Beat** as so used has no reference to **time**, and is not to be confounded with the word **Beat** as used in the chapter on **Time.**

Grace Notes, or **Embellishments,** are also called **Auxiliary** Notes. The student should observe that they are always only one degree above or one degree below the principal note, which they precede.

170. The **Slur** ⌒ or ⌣ placed over or under notes **of different pitch**, indicates that the notes over which it is placed are to be played so as to glide smoothly, one into the other, in a connected manner.

171. Dots or **Dashes** placed over or under notes thus :

indicate just the reverse of the Slur. They indicate that the notes are to be played in a **disconnected** manner, quite distinct from each other, but the dashes indicate a greater degree of distinctness than the dots.

172. Staccato is an Italian word, meaning **distinct, separated,** and is often used instead of the dots or dashes.

173. The mark ＜ indicates a gradual **increase** of tone or loudness.

The term **Crescendo** is used to signify the same thing.

The mark ＞ indicates a gradual **decrease** of tone or loudness.

Decrescendo and **Diminuendo** are used to signify the same thing. Sometimes these two signs are combined in a single note or over a number of notes thus, ＜＞. They are then termed a **Swell**, and indicate a gradual increase of tone from the beginning up to the point where the two signs meet, and then a gradual decrease of tone up to the point where the second part of the sign ends.

Many other terms will be found explained in the following alphabetical lists, No. 1 of which contains only terms relating to **Pace**, and No. 2 terms relating to **Expression and Style**, this arrangement being thought more convenient for the sake of comparison.

174. LIST 1.—TERMS RELATING TO PACE.

Adagio.—Slow.

Adagissimo.—Very slow. (Mark the superlative force of the termination **issimo.** You will often meet with it.)

Adagio Non Troppo.—Not too slow.

Allegro.—Lively, brisk, cheerful.

Allegretto.—A **Diminutive** of **Allegro,** meaning therefore, not so brisk as **Allegro.** (Mark the **Diminutive** effect of the termination **etto.** You will often meet with it.)

Allegrettino.—A **Diminutive** of **Allegretto,** meaning therefore, not so lively as **Allegretto.** (Observe the **Diminutive** effect of the termination **ino.**)

Allegrissimo.—Superlative of **Allegro,** meaning therefore, **very** brisk, **very** lively, **very** cheerful.

Andante.—Slowly and steadily, with easy motion, and without interruption.

Andantino.—A **Diminutive** of **Andante,** therefore slower than **Andante.**

A Tempo.—In strict time. After a departure from the regular time, these words mark the point at which there must be a return to it.

Assai.—Very (placed after the term it modifies).

Grave.—Grave, very slow, majestical.

Largo.—Slow, solemn, but broad and massive in character.

Largo Assai.—Very slow.

Larghetto.—**Diminutive** of **Largo.** Not so slow as **Largo.**

Larghissimo.—Superlative of **Largo,** therefore meaning **very** slow.

Lento.—Slow.

Lentissimo.—Superlative of **Lento,** and meaning **very** slow.

Listesso Tempo.—In the same time. Generally used when there is a change from $\frac{6}{8}$ time to $\frac{2}{4}$ (both two beats in the bar) and when it is intended that the **beats** in the latter case are to proceed at the same rate as in the former case.

Meno Mosso.—A little slower (not gradually).

Moderato.—Moderately quick.

Piu Mosso.—A little faster (not gradually).

Presto.—Quick.

Prestissimo.—Superlative of **Presto.** Very quick. As quick as possible.

Ritenuto.—Holding back (at once).

Stringendo.—Rapidly increasing the pace.

Tempo Primo.—In the first or original time.

You will notice on studying the foregoing terms that there are several terms expressing **slow,** and several expressing **quick,** &c., and that there are several degrees of quickness and slowness.

No attempt has been made to settle the degrees of quickness or slowness, except in the case of terms that are Augmentatives or Diminutives of other terms.

Composers do not all use the terms in exactly the same sense, that is, to indicate precisely the same pace.

As the Metronomic sign indicating pace could be used not only at the beginning of a piece, but could be repeated and varied at any desired points throughout the piece, it is to be hoped that at some future time the majority, if not all, the foregoing terms will be disused, and the Metronomic sign more freely used.

175 List 2.

Terms relating to Expression and Style.

A Bene Placito.—At pleasure, either as regards **Time** or Embellishments.

Accelerando.—Gradually increasing in rapidity of pace.

Accompagnamento.—Accompaniment.

———**Ad Lib.**—Accompaniment, that may be dispensed with or performed **at pleasure.**

———**Obligato.**—Accompaniment indispensable, that is, that cannot be omitted without marring the effect.

Ad Libitum.—See Art. 164.

Affettuoso.—Tenderly, pathetically.

Agitato.—In a hurried or agitated manner.

Animato.—In an **animated** style.

A Poco.—By degrees, gradually.

A Poco A Poco.—By little and little.

A Poco Piu Lento. — A little more slowly. See **Piu.** See **Lento.**

Arpeggio.—The notes of a chord played or sung in *succession*, instead of simultaneously.

Ben Marcato.—Well marked, that is with distinct accent.

Bene Placito.—At pleasure. See **A Bene Placito.** Also **Ad Lib.**

Calando.—Gradually diminishing the tone and slackening the pace.

Cantabile.—Capable of being sung. In a smooth, graceful, singing style.

Con Brio.—With fire and vivacity.

Con Espressione.—With expression.

Con Moto.—With animated movement.

Con Tenerezza.—With tenderness.

Crescendo.—Gradually increasing in tone. See Art. 173.
Dal Segno.—See Art. 165.
Decrescendo.—Gradually decreasing in tone. See Art. 173.
Delicato.—Delicately.
Delicatissimo.—**Very** delicately (superlative of Delicato).
Diluendo.—Gradually dying away till the tone is no longer heard.
Diminuendo.—Same as **Decrescendo**, which see.
Dolce.—Softly, sweetly.
Dolcissimo.—Superlative of **Dolce.**
Espressivo.—Expressively, with great expression.
Forte.—Loud, strong.   (Abbreviated f.)
Fortissimo.—**Very** loud. (,,   ff.)
Forte Possible.—As loud as possible.
Fine.—The end.
Glissando.—In a gliding manner. See **Slur.**
Grazioso.—Graceful, elegant.
Il Fine.—The end.
Il Piu.—The most.
Il Piu Forte Possible—As loud as possible. See **Forte.**
Il Piu Piano Possible.—As soft as possible. See **Piano.**
Lacrimoso.—Sad, mournful.
Legato.—In a smooth connected manner.
Legatissimo.—Superlative of **Legato.**
Leggiero.—Lightly.
Lentando.—Getting slower.
Lunga Pausa.—A long pause. See ⌒, Art. 164.
Maestoso.—Majestical, dignified.
Maestosissimo.—Superlative of **Maestoso.**
Marcato.—Marked, as to accent.
Marcatissimo.—Superlative of **Marcato.**
Mezzo.—Medium, moderate.

Mezzo Forte.—Moderately loud
Mezzo Piano.—Moderately soft.
Molto.—Much, extremely.
Obligato.—Indispensable. (Referring to the Accompaniment.)
Pesante.—With weight and power, ponderous.
Piano.—Soft. (Abbreviated p.)
Pianissimo.—Superlative of **Piano.** Very soft. (Abbreviated pp.)
Piu.—More.
Piu Piano.—More softly.
Piu Forte.—More loudly.
Rallentando.—Time getting gradually slower.
Ritardando.—Retarding or delaying the time (gradually).
Rinf. or Rf.—Contraction of **Rinforzando** or **Rinforzato.**
Rinforzando.—A reinforcement of tone **after a diminution.**
Rinforzato.—Same as **Rinforzando.**
Sempre.—Always. **Sempre Staccato. Sempre piano.**
Sf. or Sfz.—Contraction of **Sforzando** or **Sforzato.**
Sforzando.—With force. (Referring to one particular note.)
Sforzato.—Same as **Sforzando.**
Slentando.—Synonymous with **Rall.** Becoming slower.
Smorzando.—Dying away.
Sostenuto.—Sustained. Often applied to passages.
Staccato.—Detached, separate. See Art. 172.
Staccatissimo.—Superlative of **Staccato.**
Tanto.—As much.
Tardando.—Same as **Ritardando**, which see.
Tempo.—Time.
Tempo Ordinario.—Ordinary time.
Tempo Rubato.—Temporary deviation from strict time, by taking time from one note to give to another, but leaving the value of a bar unaffected thereby.
Tempo di Capella.—In the time of Church Music.

Tempo di Valse.—In waltz time.

Tempo Giusto.—In just, in exact time.

Tenuto.—Held, sustained. Often applied to single notes.

Tranquillo.—Tranquil, peaceable.

Troppo.—Too much; **non troppo piano,** not too soft; **non troppo forte,** not too loud.

Tutta, Tutte, Tutti, Tutto.—All; referring to either the choir, or the orchestra, or it may be used in such expressions as **Tutta Forza,** all the force possible.

Vivace.—Lively, brisk.

Vivacissimo.—Superlative of **Vivace.**

CHAPTER VIII.

INVERSION OF INTERVALS.

176. If in any interval such as D to A, Fig. (*a*) in the margin, we take the lower note D, and place it above the A, as in Fig. (*b*) in the margin, we are said to **invert** the interval, so that the interval A to D is called the **inversion** of D to A.

Or, if we had taken the upper note, A, and placed it below the D, as in Fig. (*c*) in the margin, we should have inverted the interval D to A, and obtained as its **inversion** A to D, just as before, only at a different pitch.

Hence there are two ways of inverting an interval.

(*a*) By placing the lower note above the upper note.

(*b*) By placing the upper note below the lower note.

The following shows the interval F to C inverted in both of these ways, and in each case we get C to F as the inversion.

Any interval can be inverted similarly, even if the lower note be on the Bass Staff and the upper one on the Treble Staff.

177. The following shows the inversion of each kind of interval from a Second to a Seventh, in one or other, but not both of these ways, the figures indicate the kind of interval **before** and **after** inversion.

You should now take any other note than G, write on it each interval from a second to a seventh, then invert each, and you will find intervals the same as those given above.

On examination of the given intervals and their inversions you will find that:—

A Second becomes a Seventh on inversion.
A Third ,, Sixth ,,
A Fourth ,, Fifth ,,
A Fifth ,, Fourth ,,
A Sixth ,, Third ,,
A Seventh ,, Second ,,

It will help you to remember this if you will observe that the interval and its inversion together make nine; thus, 2 and 7, 3 and 6, &c. Octaves cannot be inverted.

Besides the change in **kind** of interval just noticed, if you take the trouble to count the value of several intervals and their inversions, you will find that **Intervals change their quality on Inversion.**

A Major Interval becomes a Minor on being inverted.
A Minor ,, Major ,,
An Augmented ,, Diminished ,,
A Diminished ,, an Augmented ,,

A Perfect Interval remains Perfect on being inverted.

Hence a Perfect Fifth becomes a Perfect Fourth, and *vice versâ*.

CHAPTER IX.

Chords, and their Inversions.

The Figuring of Chords.

178. All Sounds are produced by the vibrations of particles of the air ; these vibrating particles coming in contact with certain parts of the ear produce upon us the effect which we call Sound.

There are various ways of causing the air to vibrate : one very commonly used being to cause a string to vibrate in the air, the vibrations of the string imparting a like motion to the particles of air with which the string comes in contact.

The **shorter the string** is, the more rapid will be the vibrations, and the **higher will be the pitch** of the sound ; but the **longer the string** the slower will be the vibrations, and **the lower the pitch** of the sound.

179. If you stretch any string, fasten it firmly, and by touching it, cause it to vibrate, if you watch it carefully you will observe that not only does the string vibrate for the whole of its length, but certain portions of the length, as $\frac{1}{2}$, $\frac{1}{3}$, &c., vibrate at a different rate from, and independently of, the whole string. The same is, of course, the case with the particles of air in contact with the whole of the string, and with the various sections of it, and a similar result follows if the vibrations be produced otherwise than by a string. The longer the string you take for this experiment, the more clearly will you see the effects described.

180. From what has been said in Art. 178, you will understand that if the whole string by vibrating produces a certain sound ; $\frac{1}{2}$ or $\frac{1}{3}$ of its length vibrating separately will produce a different sound and of higher pitch, so that when the string is made to vibrate for the whole of its length, there is produced not merely one sound but several.

181. Under ordinary circumstances, you cannot hear all the sounds thus produced, but under favourable circumstances you can hear clearly and distinctly three or four different sounds.

In a large hall, favourably constructed for hearing, and in which there is perfect silence, and consequently little or no vibration of the air, if you hear a low deep note struck upon an organ, or a grand piano, you can hear the additional sounds just referred to; the combination of sounds is agreeable, and the effect pleasing to the ear, so pleasing that artists very early attempted to discover, and succeeded in discovering, what were those additional sounds thus produced, with the object of copying Nature in the production of agreeable combinations of sound, or Harmonies, as they are called in Art. 2.

182. It was found that the chief of the notes thus produced by Nature from any one note were :—

a. The octave of the given note, and the octave above that again.

b. The note a fifth above the given note.

c. The note a third above the given note.

The original note is usually called a Prime, and the notes produced from it are called by various names, Overtones and Acute Harmonics being, perhaps, most generally used.

It is to be observed, however, that other notes besides those given arise naturally from any given note, but as stated these are the **chief** ones.

It is also to be observed, that the thirds and fifths are Compound Intervals, but for present purposes that does not matter; we only want to see what Nature suggests as the proper notes to sound together to form Harmony, and we find this to be **any given note; its third; its fifth; and its octave.**

183. Representing this within the compass of one octave in each case, and forming a harmony on each note of the scale, we get the following :—

Any note, with its third, fifth, and octave written above it, as in the foregoing example, forms what is called a **Chord.** It is hardly necessary to remind you that when music is written in four parts, the notes of the chords given above would be placed some on the Bass, and some on the Treble Staff, and not all on the Treble as they are written here.

You will find it very useful to commit to memory the notes of each chord as given above, thus :—C, E, G, C; D, F, A, D; E, G, B, E; F, A, C, F; G, B, D, G; A, C, E, A; B, D, F, B, as these are the notes which you will always find going together when music is written in four parts. (This latter statement will be modified a little when you study Harmony.)

184. When written as in Art. 183, that is, the note with its third, fifth and octave written above it, the chord is called a **Common Chord;** when written with the third and fifth only, above the given note, omitting the octave, the chord is called a **Triad,** from the fact of its containing two **intervals,** each being a **third,** as in each of the following :—

Triads.

Intervals like those in the foregoing examples, in which the upper note of the lower interval is the same as the lower note of the upper interval, are called **Conjunct.** In the triad C, E, G, the upper note of the interval C to E is E ; but this E is also the lower note of the interval E to G ; so these are **Conjunct Intervals.** Hence it may be said that a **triad** is made up of two **Conjunct Thirds.**

In each of the triads and common chords written above and in Art. 183, the lower note is said to **bear** the **chord** written on it, and a note which has thus a third and a fifth written above it, whether with or without the octave, is called the **root** of the chord, or of the triad.

185. By referring to Art. 110 you will see what notes of a scale bear a Major Third interval, and by reference to Art. 112 you will see what notes of a scale bear a Perfect Fifth interval. A comparison of the two will show you that when the third is Major, the fifth on the same root is always Perfect.

When the root of any common chord, or triad, bears a Major Third and Perfect Fifth, the chord or triad is called a **Major Common Chord**, or a **Major Triad**. For examples see the chords and triads on C, F, and G, in Arts. 183 and 184.

When the root of any common chord, or triad, bears a Minor Third and Perfect Fifth, the chord or triad is called a **Minor Common Chord** or **Minor Triad**. For examples see the chords and triads on D, E, A, in Arts. 183 and 184.

When the root bears a Minor Third and a Diminished Fifth, the chord or triad is called **Diminished**. For examples see the chord and triad on B, in Arts. 183 and 184.

186. If we take any of the triads above given, as for example, G, B, D, and count from the root G to B, we find the interval is a third, and counting again from G to D we find the interval is a fifth. Both these intervals are indicated by the figures 3 and 5 in diagram (*a*), the root G being figured 1; but when figures are used the 1 is omitted and the 5 and 3 are written underneath, as shown in (*b*), the figures being understood to signify that there are intervals of a third and a fifth respectively formed by the upper notes with the lower note, but no indication is given or intended of the interval formed by the upper notes among themselves.

Moreover, either the third or the fifth may be compound, as the third is in (c), and no other figuring is necessary to indicate that.

A chord written and figured as in either (a), (b) or (c) is spoken of as a **Five-three** chord, or a **Three-five** chord, and is said to be in **fundamental position**, that is, with the root in the lowest part.

187. We are said to **invert a chord**, or triad, if we invert either of the intervals (see Art. 176) made by the third or the fifth with the root of the chord.

Thus in the five-three chord G, B, D (*Fig. a*), if we invert the third, that is the interval G to B, putting the third,

that is B, in the lowest part, which can be done as in either (b), (c) or (d) we get the two upper notes now making intervals of a third and a sixth respectively with the lower note.

Either (b), (c) or (d) then is an **inversion of a common chord**, and when, as is done here, the third in the common chord is put in the lowest part, the inversion is called a **first inversion** of the common chord.

Such a position of a chord is spoken of as a **six-three** chord, and figured $\frac{6}{3}$ underneath the chord thus:—
and not with the figures alongside the notes, as in the diagrams given above.

Observe carefully that B does not become the root of the chord by being put in the lowest part; this is the chord of G still, and G remains the root, even if it be in the highest part.

Observe also, that as stated in Art. 186 the figures here have no reference to the interval which the two upper notes, D and G, now make with one another; that is not thought of; what is of importance and what is indicated by the figures is the interval made by each of the upper notes with that now in the lowest part.

188. Now suppose we take the same ⁶⁄₃ chord, G, B, D, and invert the fifth, that is the interval made by the D with G as is done in each of the three forms (*b*), (*c*) and (*d*),

in each of which the D is in the lowest part, and if we now count the interval made by each of the upper notes with the D, we find that one is a **Sixth**, the other is a **Fourth**.

Either (*b*), (*c*) or (*d*) is another inversion of a common chord, and when, as is done here, the fifth of the common chord is put in the lowest part, the inversion of the common chord is called the **Second Inversion**.

A chord in such a position is spoken of as a **Six-four** chord, and is figured ⁶⁄₄, the figures being placed underneath, thus :— and not alongside the notes as shown above.

Observe carefully again, the figures have reference to the intervals made by the upper notes with the note in the lowest part, and have no reference to the interval formed by the upper notes one with another.

189. Even when the chord is inverted it is very necessary to bear in mind what the **root** of the chord is.

In the case of the **First Inversion** the third is placed in the lowest part, but you learned in Art. 177 that a third on inversion becomes a sixth, hence in a **six-three** chord the note that forms a sixth with the lowest part, that is, the six in the ⁶⁄₃ chord, is really the **root** of the chord. (See the diagrams in Art. 187.)

In the case of the **Second Inversion** the fifth is put in the lowest part; but you learned that a fifth becomes a fourth on inversion, hence in the ⁶⁄₄ chord, the four is really the root of the chord. (See the diagrams in Art. 188.)

190. Sometimes a single note is given to you as in the diagram (*a*) with certain figures underneath, and you are asked to write the chord indicated. In this case the given note is G, and the given figures are ⁶₄, all you have  to do is to write a fourth above G, and also a sixth above G, as in diagram (*b*), and this you may do without any regard to the relative positions of the fourth and sixth. In this case the fourth is C and the sixth is E; here the C is written on the third space, but it might have been written on the second leger line above the staff, the E being still left where it is in the fourth space.

Every ⁶₄ chord is the second inversion of some other chord, and this is one also.

What, then, is the root of the chord? By reference to Art. 189 you will see that the fourth is in such a case the root. Hence the root is C, and this is the second inversion of the chord of C, the notes of this chord being C, E, G.

Similarly you may be given a note as in (*c*) with the figures ⁶₃, and you may be asked to complete the chord indicated.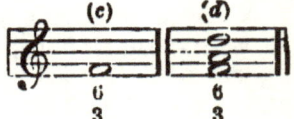

Here the given note is F: the figures indicate that you are to write a third and a sixth above the F: this you see done in (*d*). This being a ⁶₃ chord is a **first inversion** of some chord.

What is the root of the chord in this case? In a first inversion the third is placed in the lowest part, and you learned in Art. 177 that a third becomes a sixth on inversion, so that the sixth here is really the root of the chord; but D is the sixth; hence D is the root of this chord, so this is a first inversion of the chord of D, the notes of this chord being D, F, A.

Similarly you can tell the root in any other case, and you should exercise yourself well in doing so. If a chord be not figured, you can easily count the interval which each note makes with that in the lowest part, and figure accordingly yourself.

CHAPTER X.

Voice Training.

191. How can I cure this flattening? is the sincere cry of many a teacher in reference to the School Singing. The causes of flattening are numerous, the following are the principal:—

Neglect of Voice Training Exercises.

Forcing up the lower registers beyond their limits.

Want of interest, inattention, laziness, fatigue.

Bad posture in singing.

Want of ventilation.

Singing in a loud coarse tone throughout.

The first two are by far the most common. The teacher who wishes to have good, refined singing, with the pitch sustained, should proceed as follows:—

192. Take the worst singers and place them in the front row, select the best singers and place them at the back, let the class stand at ease; now give a sound about G and ask class to sing it to koo, the k promotes a prompt "attack," and the oo brings the tone forward in the mouth instead of back in the throat. When this has been done two or three times fairly well, the tone being good and the singing sounding as if by one voice, let the class sing it to "ah," the vowel the same as in "father," the **mouth being well opened.** Take care the tone is forward as it was in koo, not guttural, throaty or harsh, but smooth, fluty and pleasant. The pitch may now be changed to any note between the two C's.

The following exercises should follow, Key C and D. Let every exercise be first sung to the Sol-fa notes:—

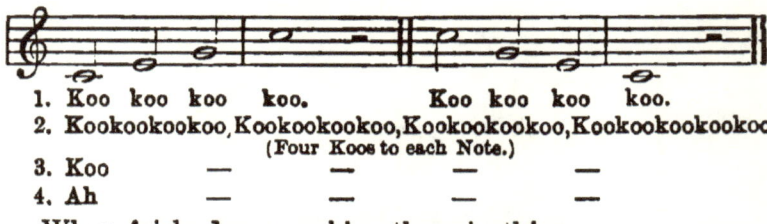

1. Koo koo koo koo.   Koo koo koo koo.
2. Kookookookoo, Kookookookoo, Kookookookoo, Kookookookookoo
   (Four Koos to each Note.)
3. Koo   —   —   —   —
4. Ah   —   —   —   —

When fairly done combine them in this way.

193. Breathing exercises are useful, as children will not be so likely to spoil a word or phrase by taking breath in the middle; the tone will be better, and a long note or phrase can be sustained without fatigue, thus the exercises materially assist in sustaining the pitch. Teacher should give a sound about A or G, ask class to take a deep breath while he raises the pointer, and expel it slowly to "ah" while he counts, say, ten at first at M. 60, gradually increasing the number of beats as the class gains power.

194. The general rules of voice training in schools are:— Try to secure a forward quality of tone, not throaty or guttural, see that the thick register is not forced up, especially by boys; look after the posture of children, a good opening of the mouth, and a sharp and clear pronunciation. Use principally chordal exercises, and take both voice and breathing exercises at the beginning of the singing lesson. It is of the greatest assistance for the teacher to be able to give a good pattern of what he wants.

195. Voice training is much more effectual if taken frequently for a short time than if taken occasionally for a long time.

By all means avoid the use of an instrument, especially a harmonium, in teaching singing, it is much worse than useless.

This should follow at a succeeding lesson in Keys D up

to G, *i.e.*, D, E♭, E, F, F♯, G.   The last exercise had better precede this at each lesson.

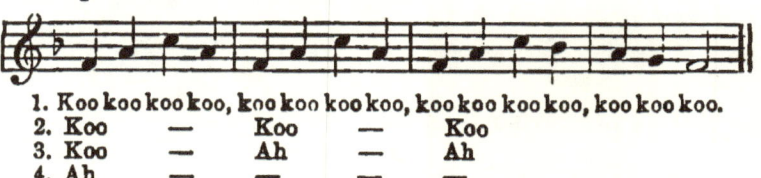

1. Koo koo koo koo, koo koo koo koo, koo koo koo koo, koo koo koo.
2. Koo — Koo — Koo
3. Koo — Ah — Ah
4. Ah — — — —

These will follow a week or two later, Keys C up to F.

196. COMPASS—

Infants.		 to
Children and Women	Trebles under ten years of age.	 to
	Altos under ten years of age.	 to
	Trebles above ten years of age.	 to
	Altos above ten years of age.	 to
Men	Tenors 8ve lower.	 to
	Basses.	to

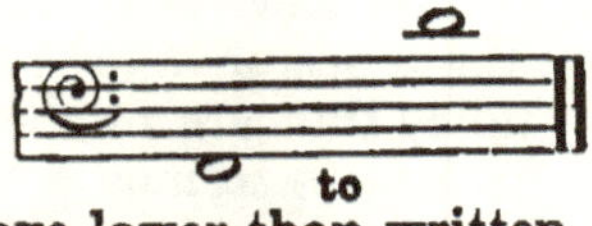

Note that Tenor Compass is an octave lower than written.

L

As soon as a boy's voice breaks he should stop singing, or he will spoil the singing of the rest, and perhaps injure his own voice.

197. Classifying Trebles and Altos—

If the singing is to be really good in a school it is very necessary that the children be sorted into treble and alto, not according to their sex or classes, but according to each child's natural qualifications. If a child with an alto voice tries to reach the higher notes of treble he will flatten and bring others down with him, and if a child with a light soprano voice tries to sing alto, it will be ineffective and probably spoil the voice. In many cases the teacher will be able to tell by the speaking voice of the child which part he should take. In other cases, the compass is not to be the guide, but let teacher give G and children sing up; those who can lightly and easily run up to upper F^1 or G^1 will be treble, those whose rounder, fuller tones are below the G will be altos.

In a competition of children's choirs the following would be the heads under which marks would be given: tune, time, quality and volume of tone, expression, pronunciation, keeping the pitch, discipline of singers and also of conductor.

The singing in infant schools should, as a rule, be piano.
Standards I. and II., mezzo piano ⎫
Standards III. and above, mezzo ⎬ as a rule.

198. Registers—

The sounds of the human voice are not all produced by the same mechanism of the vocal ligaments, the positions of these are changed as we ascend or descend. The series of notes that are produced by any one position of the vocal ligaments is termed a "Register."

The following is the compass of the registers of women and children :—

199. These registers are described by some writers and trainers as "chest," "medium," "head," &c., but the above names are best, as they describe the mechanism by which the tones are produced. The place where the voice changes from one register to another is termed a "break," and that between upper thick and lower thin the "great break."

A most common cause of coarse and flat singing is forcing up the lower registers beyond their limits, especially forcing the upper thick even as high as D¹, neglecting the thin register altogether. This is mainly done by boys, and especially those who shout and play in the streets. The teacher must resolutely determine to cure this evil by invariably insisting on **soft** singing on C¹ and above till the fault is cured. The following is a good exercise for the purpose :—

Insist on soft singing, ask boys to try and sing like the girls; in mixed schools let the girls sing and boys imitate.

This exercise follows when above has been correctly done a few times.

200. In all succeeding exercises and songs keep a look out for all notes about E, F and G; tell children that the notes at that pitch can be produced in two ways, and that you want the soft flute-like tone. Girls sometimes need these exercises, but boys always do. Both boys and girls need watching to see that they enter the small register on high G¹. Again insist that the tone shall be soft, bird-like, and if necessary give above exercise in Key G, the highest note piano.

It will be noticed that all above exercises ascend by leaps; this is because an ascending scale passage strongly tempts one to carry the register up too far. There is no objection to a descending scale passage, as no harm is done by bringing a register down below its limits, but this is rarely done.

When good tone has become a habit, and the thick register no longer forced up, the following exercises may be used to secure agility, taken slowly and gradually increasing the speed, Keys E♭ up to A.

Longer exercises, either chordal or stepwise, may follow, always remembering that chordal exercises are the safest. Don't forget this if asked at an examination what kind of voice exercises are best.

It is a good plan to take a verse of a hymn or song which can be sung without book, let it be practised till it is sung with good tone, then divide class into four sections, and let each section sing one line one after another without pause.

In this and in other ways which the inventiveness of the teacher will suggest, the question, "How can I cure this flattening, and secure good tone?" will be effectively answered.

QUESTIONS ON THE CHAPTERS.

All Students using this book are recommended to test their knowledge of any chapter before leaving it, by answering the questions here given.

QUESTIONS ON CHAPTER I.

1 *a*. Give the alphabetic and syllabic names of the notes, up and down, beginning with **C**, or **Do**.

  b. Give the same extending over two octaves, up and down.

2 *a*. Give the alphabetic names of alternate notes from **C** upwards for two octaves.

  b. Give the same downwards for two octaves.

3 *a*. Give the syllabic names of alternate notes, beginning with **Do** and proceeding upwards.

  b. Give the same beginning with **Do** and proceeding downwards.

4 *a*. Give the syllabic names of alternate notes, beginning with **Do** and proceeding upwards for two octaves.

  b. Give the same downwards for two octaves.

5 *a*. What are the syllabic names corresponding to D, F, A, C, E, G, B respectively?

  b. What are the alphabetic names corresponding to Mi, So, Si, Re, Fa, La, Do, respectively?

6 *a*. Write a Great Staff; mark the fourth, seventh and tenth lines, also the third, sixth and eighth spaces.

  b. Write a Great Staff again, making the sixth line a dotted line.

7 *a.* Write the same again, omitting the sixth line altogether, and numbering the lines and spaces of the upper and lower halves of it separately and independently.

b. Write separately the upper half of the Great Staff, that is, write the Treble Staff, with Clef.

8 *a.* Write a note on each line of the Treble Clef and name each note written.

b. Write a note on each space of the Treble Clef and name each note written.

9 *a.* Write the lower half of the Great Staff, that is, write the Bass Staff, with Clef.

b. Write a note on each line of the Bass Staff and name each note written.

c. Write a note on each space of the Bass Staff and name each note written.

10 *a.* Write the Great Staff and show the position of Middle C on it.

b. Write the Treble Staff and write Middle C on it.

c. Write the Bass Staff and write Middle C on it.

11 *a.* Write two leger lines **above** the Treble Staff, place notes on them and on the new spaces formed, and name each of those notes.

b. Write two leger lines **below** the Treble Staff, place notes on them and on the spaces formed, and name each of those notes.

12 *a.* Write two leger lines **above** the Bass Staff, place notes on them and on the spaces formed, and name each of those notes.

b. Write two leger lines **below** the Bass Staff, place notes on them and on the new spaces formed, and name each of those notes.

13 *a.* Write on the Treble Staff the following notes:— E, B, G, C, F, A, D.

b. Write on the Bass Staff the following notes:— A, F, D, G, C, B, E.

14 *a.* Write these notes an octave higher on the Bass Staff:—

  b. Write them on the Treble Staff same pitch as here given.

15 *a.* Write these notes an octave lower on the Treble Staff.

  b. Write them an octave lower on the Bass Staff.

  c. Write them same pitch on the Bass Staff.

16 *a.* Name the following notes on the Treble Staff:—

  b. Name the following notes on the Bass Staff:—

17 *a.* Write the Great Staff all in dotted lines except the five lines used for the Alto Staff, for which you are to use black lines.

  b. Write the Alto Staff with Clef.

  c. Write Middle C on the Alto Staff.

18 *a.* Write any four notes on the Treble Staff, and then write the same notes, same pitch, on the Alto Staff.

  b. Write any four notes on the Alto Staff, and then write the same four, same pitch, on the Treble Staff.

  c. Name the notes on the lines and spaces of the Alto Staff.

19 *a.* Write the Great Staff all in dotted lines except the five lines used for the Tenor Staff, for which you are to use black lines.

  b. Write the Tenor Staff with Clef.

  c. Write Middle C on the Tenor Staff.

20 *a.* Name the notes on the lines and spaces of the Tenor Staff.

   b. Write any four notes on the Tenor Staff, and then write the same notes, same pitch, on the Bass Staff.

   c. Write any four notes on the Bass Staff, and then write the same notes, same pitch, on the Tenor Staff.

21. Write a Great Staff, and place each of the following on it in proper position :—

    G clef, F clef, C clef Alto, C clef Tenor.

22. What is meant by **Full Score** and **Short Score** respectively?

23. Describe in words, and show by means of a diagram the usual compass of the Treble, Alto, Tenor, and Bass voices respectively.

24. Re-write the following in the Bass Clef, to sound **one** octave lower than here written :—

25. Re-write the following in the Treble Clef to sound **one** octave higher :—

26. Re-write the following in the Bass Clef to sound **two** octaves lower :—

27. Re-write the following in the Treble Clef to sound **two** octaves higher :—

28. Re-write the following at the **same pitch** in the Bass Clef:—

29. Re-write the following at the **same pitch** in the Treble Clef:—

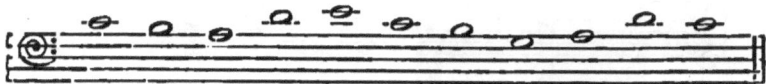

30. Write the following at the **same pitch** in the Treble Clef, in the Alto Clef, and in the Tenor Clef:—

QUESTIONS ON CHAPTER II.

31. On the second line of the staff place the following notes:—Crotchet, Semiquaver, Minim, Demisemiquaver, Semibreve, Quaver.

32. Under each of the following notes write its **time** name:—

33. On a staff write the rests corresponding to the following notes:—Semibreve, Minim, Crotchet, Quaver, Semiquaver, Demisemiquaver, Semidemisemiquaver.

34. Give the **time** names of the notes corresponding to the following rests:—

35. Alongside each of the following notes write the corresponding rest :—

36. Alongside each of the following rests write the corresponding note :—

37. If a semibreve were value for 32, what would be the value of a quaver? of a crotchet? of a semidemisemiquaver?

38. If a semiquaver were value for $\frac{1}{2}$, what would be the value of a semibreve?

39. What is the effect of a dot after a note or rest?

40. What is the effect of a second dot, and of a third dot respectively, after a note or rest?

41. Without using dots write the equivalent of each of the following trebly dotted notes :—

42. Write one note of the same length as the following three :—

and one of the same length as the following two :—

43. What is meant by a Tie or Bind? Give an example of its use.

44. Set down the equivalent of a semibreve in four different ways, none of them being a mere repetition of the same note.

45. Set down the equivalent of a minim in four different ways, none of them being a mere repetition of the same note.

46. Set down the equivalent of a crotchet in four different ways, none of them being a mere repetition of the same note.
47. Set down the equivalent of a quaver in four different ways, none of them being a mere repetition of the same note.
48. What are Bar Lines?
49. What is meant by the Time Signature of a piece?
50. What is meant by C or $\frac{4}{4}$ as a time signature? Write six bars of music in the species of time indicated by that signature: give variety so that no bar will be a mere repetition of a previous bar. In this and the following questions of the same kind, you are expected to use some rests.
51. What is meant by ₵ as a time signature?
    Write four bars of music in this species of time.
52. Give a clear and full explanation of the meaning of the fraction $\frac{2}{4}$ as a time signature.
    Write six bars in this species of time.
53. Explain the meaning of $\frac{2}{8}$ as a time signature, and write six bars in this species of time.
54. Explain the meaning of $\frac{3}{8}$ as a time signature, and write six bars or measures in this species of time.
55. Explain the meaning of $\frac{3}{4}$ as a time signature, and write six bars in this species of time.
56. Explain the meaning of $\frac{3}{8}$ as a time signature, and write six bars in this species of time.
57. Explain what is meant by Duple, Quadruple, and Triple Times respectively, and give one example of each.
58. What is meant by Simple Time? Give an example.
59. What is meant by Compound Time? Give an example.
60. What is meant by $\frac{6}{4}$ as a time signature? Write four bars in this species of time, no one bar to be a mere repetition of a previous bar.

61. What is meant by $\frac{6}{8}$ as a time signature? Write four bars in this species of time, no one bar to be a mere repetition of a previous bar.

62. What is meant by $\frac{6}{16}$ as a time signature? Write four bars in this species of time, no one bar to be a mere repetition of a previous bar.

63. Explain the meaning of $\frac{12}{4}$ as a time signature, and write four bars in this species of time, no one bar to be a mere repetition of a previous bar.

64. Explain the meaning of $\frac{12}{8}$ as a time signature, and write four bars in this species of time, no one bar to be a mere repetition of a previous bar.

65. Explain the meaning of $\frac{12}{16}$ as a time signature, and write four bars in this species of time, no one bar to be a mere repetition of a previous bar.

66. Explain the meaning of $\frac{9}{4}$ as a time signature, and write four bars in this species of time, no one bar to be a mere repetition of a previous bar.

67. Explain the meaning of $\frac{9}{8}$ as a time signature, and write four bars in this species of time, no one bar to be a mere repetition of a previous bar.

68. Explain the meaning of $\frac{9}{16}$ as a time signature, and write four bars in this species of time, no one bar to be a mere repetition of a previous bar.

69. Explain the difference between Simple and Compound Time.

70. Write, side by side, three examples of different kinds of Simple Duple Time, and three of Compound Duple Time.

71. Write, side by side, three examples of different kinds of Simple Triple Time, and three of Compound Triple Time.

72. Write three examples of different kinds of Simple Quadruple Time, and three of Compound Quadruple Time.

73. Write Time Signatures to the following :—

(a)

(b)

(c)

(d)

(e)

(f)

(g)

74. Complete the following bars according to the signatures, by adding in each case a note and a rest, either or both of which may or may not be dotted :—

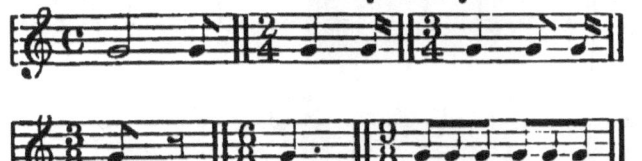

75. In each of the following exercises mark the position of the Principal Accent with ∧: of the Secondary or Subordinate Accent with ∨, and of the Sub-secondary Accent, when there is one, with + :—

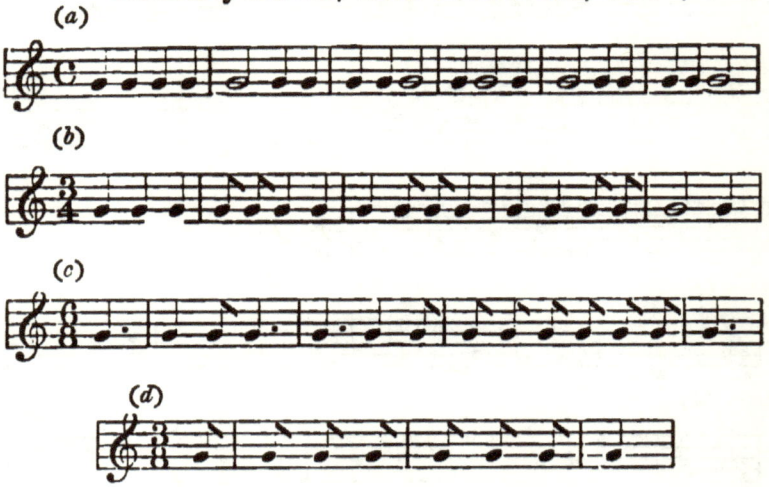

76. Explain the meanings of the following:—
  (a) M = 90 ♩; (b) ♩ = 40 M; (c) M = ♩ 120.

77. What is Syncopation? Give an example of its use.

78. What is a Triplet? Give an example.

79. Give three examples of marks or terms used to alter the strict time of a piece by prolonging one or more notes.

80. Give three examples of marks or terms used to alter the strict time of a piece by quickening the pace. (See Art. 174.)

81. Bar the following passages in accordance with the time signatures. Each passage commences a bar.

82. Add one note at the end, in the parenthesis provided, to complete each of the following bars:—

83. Add one rest at the end to complete each of the bars in question No. 82.

84. Add one note at the end to complete each of the following bars:—

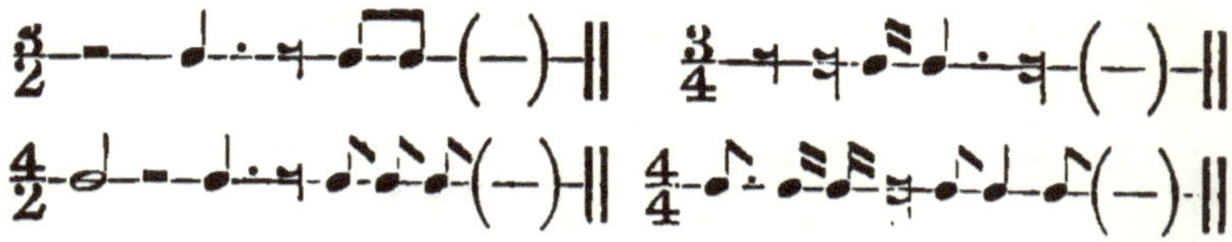

85. Add one rest at the end to complete each of the bars in question No. 84.

86. Add the time signatures to each of the following bars:—

(a)   (b)   (c)

(d)   (e)   (f)

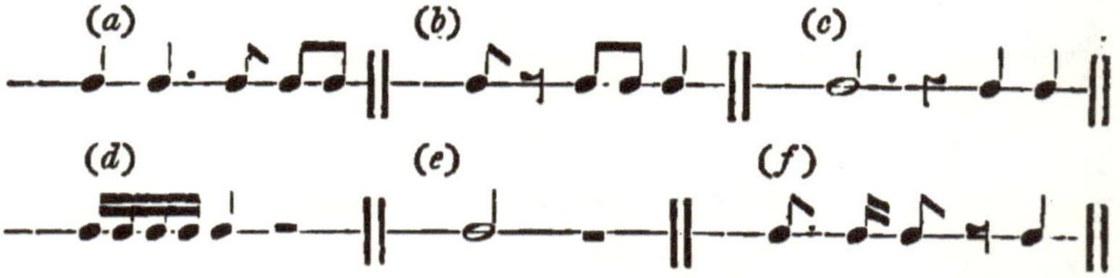

87. Bar the following passages in accordance with the time signatures. Each passage commences a bar.

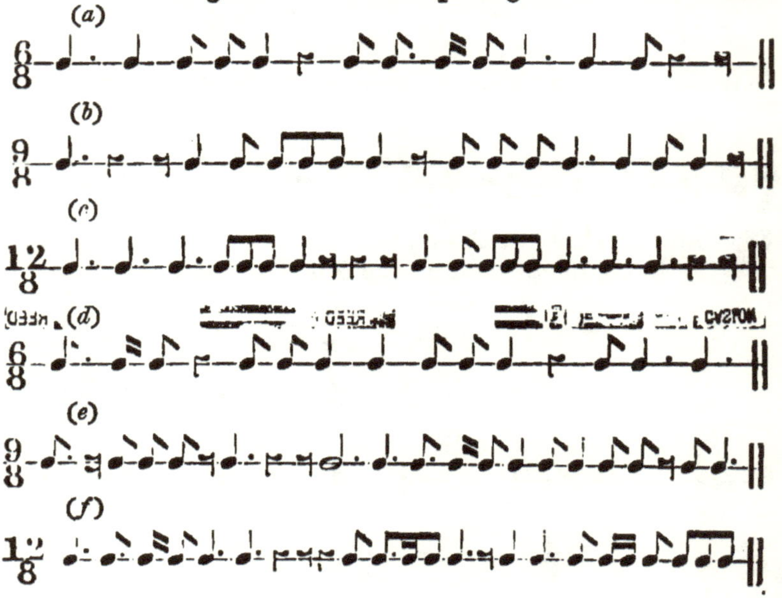

(a)

(b)

(c)

(d)

(e)

(f)

88. Add one note at the end to complete each of the following bars:—

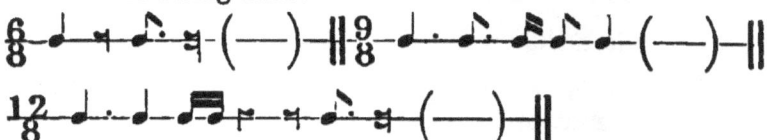

89. Add the time signatures to the following bars:—

90. Place a cross over the syncopated notes in the following passages:—

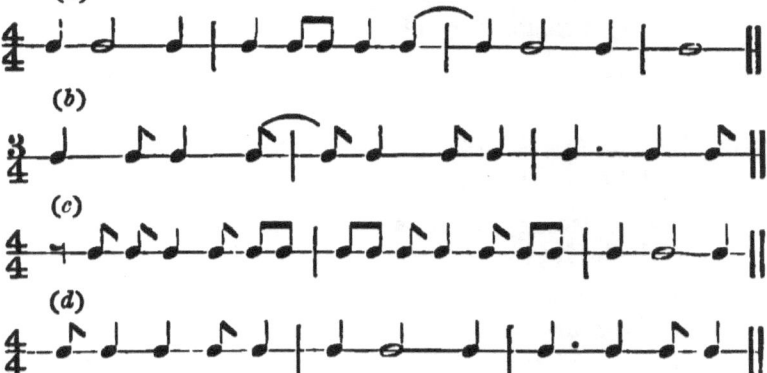

91. Explain the meanings of the following:—

♪ = M. 120; ♩ = M. 70; ♩ = M. 90; ♩. = M. 70

92. Write two bars each of 2/4, 4/4, 3/4 and 6/8 time. Insert a triplet in each bar.

QUESTIONS ON CHAPTER III.

93. What is a Tetrachord? How many Tetrachords in a scale?

94. Between what notes of a Major Scale do the tones and the semitones respectively occur?

95. Name the Keys on an instrument between which semitones occur.

96. Explain the meaning of the symbols ♯, ♭, ♮.

97. What is meant by the **Natural Order of Scale Formation?**

98. Name the Key notes, or first notes, of the various scales with sharp signatures, naming them in the natural order of scale formation.

99. Name, in the order in which they occur, the various sharps used in Key signatures.

100. From seeing the sharps in the signature of any Major Scale, how can you tell the Key?

101. Name, in the natural order of Scale formation, the Key notes of the various scales with flat signatures.

102. Name, in the order in which they occur, the various flats used in Key signatures.

103. From seeing the flats in the signature of a Major Scale, how can you tell the Key?

104. Name the Keys of which the following are the signatures:—

105. Write, in correct position on the staff, the signatures of the following Major Keys:—G; B; B♭; G♭; F♯.

106. Prefix sharps to such of the following notes as will transform the series into the scale of D.

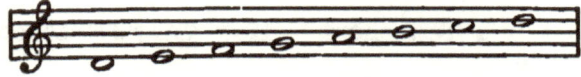

107. Prefix flats to such of the notes in Question 106 as will transform the series into the scale of D♭.

108. What alteration is necessary in the series of notes given in (*a*) and (*b*) respectively, to change these into the scales of A and A♭ respectively.

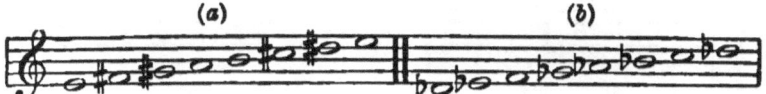

109. Name the Keys of which the following are the signatures :—

110. Write in the Treble Clef the signatures of the following Major Keys :—G, B, B♭, G♭, F♯.

111. Write in the Bass Clef the signatures of the following Major Keys :—E, A♭, A, D, F.

112. Arrange the sharps or flats of the following signatures in the customary order and position, and state for what Major Keys they stand :—

113. Arrange the following sharps and flats as in previous question.

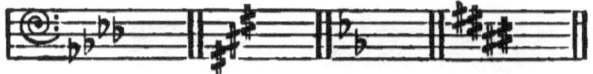

114. Write in the Treble Clef one octave of the scales of D major and G♭ major, placing the necessary sharps or flats *before the notes* and not as a signature.

115. Write on the Bass Clef, as in previous question, the scales of A♭ major and B major.

116. Write the following in the Bass Clef (adding the signature) to sound two octaves lower :—

117. Write the following in the Bass Clef (adding the signature) to sound one octave lower:—

118. Write the following in the Treble Clef (adding the signature) to sound one octave higher:—

119. Write the following in the Treble Clef (adding the signature) to sound one octave higher:—

120. Write the following in the Bass Clef (adding the signature) two octaves lower:—

121. Write the following in the Treble Clef (adding the signature) two octaves higher:—

122. Write the following in the Treble Clef (adding the signature) one octave higher:—

QUESTIONS ON CHAPTER IV.

123. What is an interval? Give an example.
124. Name the various **kinds** of Intervals. Give an example of each.
125. What is meant by the Extremes of an Interval? Give examples.
126. Name the various **qualities** of intervals.
127. What is meant by the **value** of an interval?
128. What is the value of each of the following intervals? —Major Second; Major Third; Major Sixth; Major Seventh; Minor Second; Minor Third; Minor Sixth; Minor Seventh.
129. What is the value of a Perfect Fourth? Of a Tritone Fourth? Of a Perfect Fifth? Of a Diminished Fifth? Of a Perfect Octave?
130. What notes of a scale bear Minor Seconds?
131. What notes of a scale bear Minor Thirds?
132. How many Tritone Fourths occur in any scale? On what note of the scale does the Tritone occur?
133. How many Diminished Fifths occur in a scale? And on what note of the scale does the Diminished Fifth occur?
134. Name the kind and quality of the following intervals:—

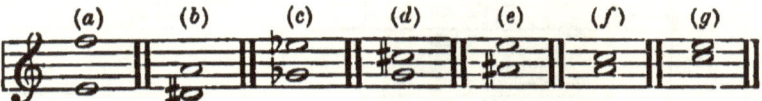

135. Write on a staff a Major Third above each of the following:—
A♭; C♯; E; B♭; G♯; D♭; F♯.
136. On a staff write a Minor Sixth above each of the notes given in Question 135.
137. On a staff write a Perfect Fifth above each of the notes in Question 135.

138. What is meant by an Augmented Interval? and what by a Diminished Interval?

139. By the use of accidentals before the upper note in each of the following:—

    change (a) into an Augmented Fifth,
             (b) into an Augmented Sixth,
             (c) into an Augmented Second,
             (d) into an Augmented Octave.

140. By the use of accidentals before the upper note in each of the following:—

    change (a) into a Diminished Third,
             (b) into a Diminished Fourth,
             (c) into a Diminished Fifth,
             (d) into a Diminished Seventh,
             (e) into a Diminished Octave.

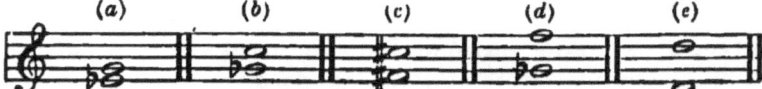

141. Name the kind and quality of the following intervals, and say in what Major Keys might each of these intervals be found:—

142. Add Major Sevenths above each of the following notes, and say in what Major Keys might each of the intervals so formed be found:—

143. Add Minor Thirds above each of the following notes, and state in what Major Keys might each of the intervals so formed be found :—

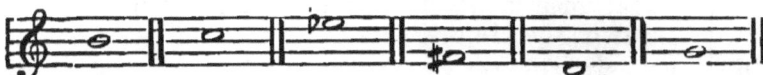

144. Write an Augmented Fourth above each of the following notes, and state in what scale might each interval so formed be found :—

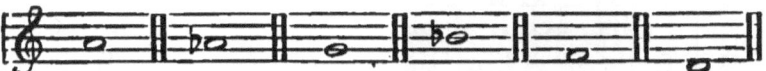

145. Write *below* (a) a Diminished Seventh ; below (b) a Diminished Fifth ; below (c) an Augmented Fourth ; below (d) a Diminished Third ; below (e) an Augmented Sixth :—

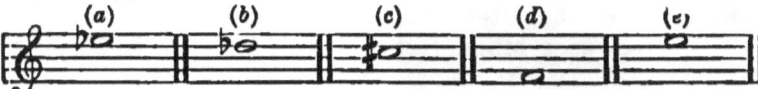

146. Write *above* (a) an Augmented Sixth ; above (b) an Augmented Fifth ; above (c) a Diminished Third ; above (d) a Major Seventh ; above (e) a Diminished Seventh :—

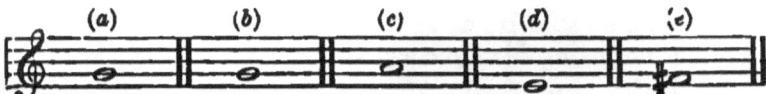

147. Write an Augmented Fifth above each of the following notes :—

Questions on Chapter V.

148. What is a Major Scale? What is a Minor Scale?

149. What do you understand by the **Relative** Minor to any Major Scale?

150. How do you tell the Relative Minor to any Major Key?

151. Where do the semitones occur in a Minor Scale in that form in which no note is altered from what it was in the Major Scale?

152. Explain the reason for the various alterations of notes that take place in the different forms of Minor Scale and point out where the semitones occur after each of these alterations.

153. Write, in at least three forms, each of the Scales A Minor and E Minor.

154. Write, in at least three forms, each of the Scales D Minor, G Minor, and C Minor.

155. Write all the Key Signatures given in Question 104: above each write the Major Key, and below each write the Minor Key of which it is the signature.

156. Name the Relative Minor Key to each of the following Major Keys:—C, G, D, A, E, B, F♯, C♯.

157. Name the Relative Minor Key to each of the following Major Keys:—C, F, B♭, E♭, A♭, D♭, G♭, C♭.

158. Name the Relative Major Key to each of the following Minor Keys:—E♭, B♭, F, G, D.

159. Name the Relative Major Key to each of the following Minor Keys:—A♯, C♯, F♯, B, E, A.

160. Write the Scale of E♭ Minor with the Major Seventh in both ascending and descending.

161. Write the Scale of D Minor with a Major Sixth in ascending and a Minor Sixth in descending. (Observe that the Raised Sixth necessarily implies the Raised Seventh also.)

162. Write the Scale of A♯ Minor with a Major Sixth and a Major Seventh in ascending, and a Minor Seventh and Minor Sixth in descending.
163. Explain the terms **Tonic Minor** and **Tonic Major**.
164. Write the Melodic Form of the Tonic Minor to E Major.
165. Write the Melodic Form of the Tonic Minor to A♭ Major.
166. What do you notice with respect to the number of flats or sharps required in the formation of any Major Scale and its Tonic Minor Melodic Form?
167. Write in the **Treble** Clef the signatures of the following Minor Keys:—C Sharp Minor, D Minor, F Sharp Minor, and G Minor.
168. Write in the **Bass** Clef the signatures of the following Minor Keys:—E Minor, C Minor, F Minor, and G Sharp Minor.
169. Write above the staff the names of the Major Keys, and below the staff the names of the Minor Keys for which the following signatures stand.

170. Write in the Treble Clef, and again in the Bass Clef, the undermentioned Scales (ascending) and their signatures:—E Minor, with the Minor Sixth and Major Seventh; G Minor, with Major Sixth and Major Seventh.
171. Write the following Scales (ascending) in the Treble Clef, and again in the Bass Clef, placing the necessary flats or sharps immediately before the notes, and **not** as a signature:—D Minor, with Minor Sixth and Major Seventh; B Minor, with Major Sixth and Major Seventh.
172. Write as in previous question, the Scales of F Sharp Minor, and B Flat Minor, with the Major Sixth and Major Seventh in each case.

173. Write in the Treble Clef, and again in the Bass Clef, the undermentioned Scales (descending) and their signatures:—C Minor, with Major Seventh and Minor Sixth; C Sharp Minor, with Major Seventh and Minor Sixth.

174. Write the Upper Tetrachord of the Scale of F Minor in three different ways.

175. Name the following intervals, and write the signature of the Minor Scale of which each interval forms a part.

176. In the following Minor Scale, point out any intervals that are not found in any Major Diatonic Scale.

177. Name the kind and quality of the following intervals, and state in what scale or scales might each be found:—

[N.B.—The Augmented Sixth does not belong to any Major or Minor Scale. It is borrowed from the Chromatic Scale.]

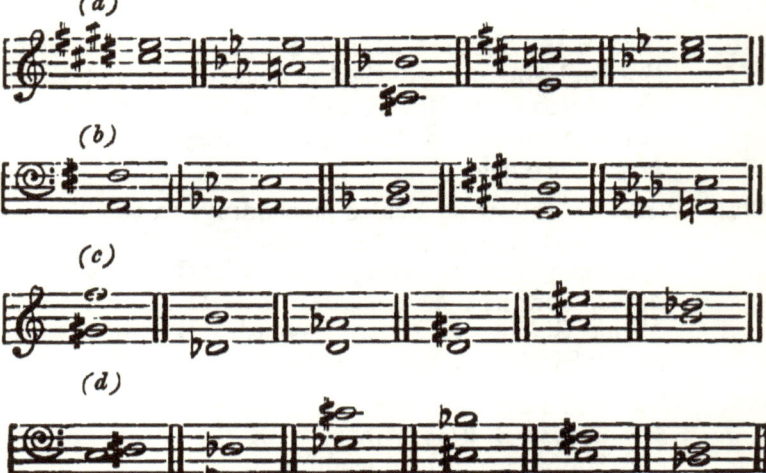

178. Write a Major Third above each of the following notes, and state in what scale or scales might the intervals so formed be found:—

179. Name the following intervals, and state in what scales might each be found:—

180. State the Key of each of the following passages. Each passage is to be considered to be in one Key throughout.

181. Re-write each of the following passages, using the proper signature.

Questions on Chapter VI.

182. What notes of a scale are called by the names Dominant, Sub-Dominant, and Leading Note, respectively?

183. What notes of a scale are called by the names Mediant, Sub-Mediant, Tonic and Super-Tonic, respectively?

184. What are the Mental Effects of the Tonic, Mediant, Dominant, and Leading Note, respectively?

185. What are the Mental Effects of the Super-Tonic, Sub-Dominant, and Sub-Mediant, respectively?

186. Give at least one example from a piece of music you have learned in which any one of the beforementioned notes produces in a striking manner the mental effect you ascribe to it.

187. Write Semibreves to show the relations named in the Major Keys indicated :—

(1) Dominant. (2) Supertonic. (3) Mediant. (4) Leading note.

188. Write Semibreves to show the relations named in the Major Keys indicated :—

(1) Sub-dominant. (2) Tonic. (3) Sub-mediant. (4) Dominant.

189. State the Major Key relation (as tonic, mediant, etc.) of the following notes :—

190. State the Major Key relation of the following notes :—

191. What is Modulation?

192. Explain the difference between Natural and Extraneous Modulation.

193. What are the relative or attendant Keys to A Major? To B♭ Major? To C♯ Minor? To F Minor?

194. Trace the Modulations in the following passages:—

195. Give an example of Modulation from any Major Key you choose to select, into its relative Minor.

196. Give two examples of Natural Modulation, in one of which the addition of a sharp to the signature is required, but in the other the removal of a sharp from the signature is required. In both instances return to the original Key before you finish.

197. Give two examples of Natural Modulation, in one of which the addition of a flat to the signature is required, but in the other the removal of a flat from the signature is required. In both instances return to the original Key before you finish.

198. What is meant by Transposition?

199. Transpose each of the following a Major Third higher :—

200. Does the Accidental in second bar in 199 (d) indicate Modulation? If so, into what Key?

201. Does the Accidental which you use to produce the same effect as that in second bar of 199 (d) indicate Modulation? If so, into what Key?

202. Transpose the following into the Scale of A ♭ Major, and again into the Scale of A Major :—

203. Transpose the following passages as indicated:—

(*a*) A Major Second lower—viz., into the Key of F Major.

(*b*) A Major Second higher—viz., into the Key of C Major.

(*c*) A Minor Second higher—viz., into the Key of B♭ Major.

(*d*) A Major Third higher—viz., into the Key of G Major.

(*e*) A Major Second higher—viz., into the Key of G Major.

(*f*) A Major Second lower—viz., into the Key of B♭ Major.

(*g*) A Minor Third lower—viz., into the Key of D Major.

(*h*) A Major Third higher—viz., into the Key of D Major.

(*i*) A Major Third higher—viz., into the Key of F♯ Minor.

(j) A Major Third lower—viz., into the Key of E♭ Minor.

204. What is meant by a Compound Interval?

205. Write a Compound Second on F; also a Compound Third on D.

206. What is meant by Transcription?

207. Transcribe (a) and (b) into ⁴⁄₄ time, (c) into ²⁄₄, and (d) into ³⁄₄ time:—

208. Transcribe (a) into ⁴⁄₄ time, (b) into ³⁄₈ time, (c) into ⁴⁄₂ time, (d) into ³⁄₄ time, (e) into ²⁄₄ time, (f) into ⁹⁄₈ time, (g) into ⁴⁄₄ time.

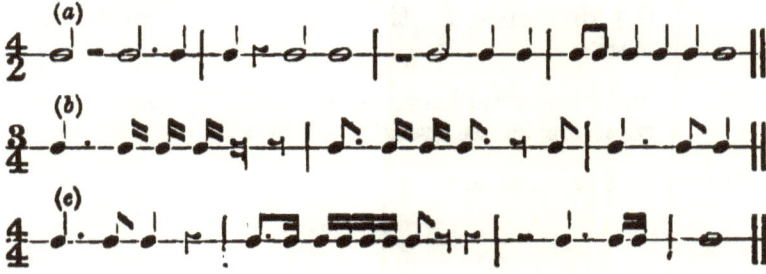

209. In the previous question transcribe (*b*) into ⅜ time, (*c*) into ⅘ time, (*f*) into ⅜ time.

Questions on Chapter VII.

210. What is a Double Bar, and what is its use?

211. What is the use of dots placed before or after a Double Bar?

212. Explain the meaning of the following:—
D. C. or Da Capo; Ad Lib.; Dal Segno.

213. What are Grace Notes? Name and give examples of the chief of them.

214. Give examples of the Slur and the Tie, and explain the difference in the meaning attached to these marks.

215. What is the meaning of the term Staccato? and what marks are used to indicate this?

216. What is a Pause?

Questions on Chapters VIII. and IX.

217. What is meant by Inverting an Interval? Give an example.

218. Invert each of the following intervals in two ways, naming the intervals here given and also those formed by inversion; state kind and quality of interval in each case:—

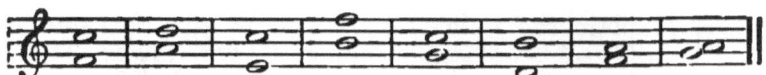

219. What is a Common Chord? and what is a Triad? Give an example of each.

220. Explain what is meant by (*a*) the First Inversion, and (*b*) the Second Inversion of a Chord. Give an example of each.

221. Write a Common Chord on each of the following notes, using both the Bass and Treble Staves for the purpose: A, E, B, F, C, G, D, and say what is the **Root** of each of these Chords.

222. Write a First Inversion of each of the following Triads, pointing out the **Root** both in the given Triad, and in the Inversion:—

223. Write a Second Inversion of each of the Triads in Question 222, pointing out the **Root** in each Inversion.

224. Complete the Chords on the following notes in the manner indicated by the figuring, and point out the **Root** of each Chord :—

225. Explain the following terms, and give an example of each :—Major Common Chord, Major Triad, Minor Common Chord, Minor Triad, Diminished Triad.

QUESTIONS ON CHAPTER X.

226. Name some causes of flattening, and how you would deal with flat singing in schools.
227. What sort of tone would you try to get rid of, and what kind would you try to secure.
228. Discuss the use and abuse of voice exercises in class singing.
229. Write a new voice exercise for lower standards with the vowels you would use.
230. What are the uses of breathing exercises?
231. Which would be most beneficial—a daily practice of five minutes' duration, or a weekly practice of forty minutes? Give reasons for your answers.
232. What principles would guide you in classifying children's voices?
233. What is meant by Registers?
234. Name the Register that needs most training in boys' voices, and state briefly the way to cultivate it.
235. Name the Compass of the following :—Infants, Trebles over ten, Basses.
236. What is the average upward limit of children's voices—(*a*) of trebles, (*b*) of altos?

237. Re-write the following phrase at a pitch in which it will be adapted to the Compass (*a*) of an average young treble and again (*b*) of an average well-developed young alto :—

238. Re-write the following phrase as in the previous question :—

239. In schools where classes are grouped for singing, what objection is there to one class singing Alto and another class singing Treble ?

240. In a competition of choirs under what heads would you give marks ?

ADDITIONAL QUESTIONS ON THE VARIOUS CHAPTERS.

241. Copy out the following melody and write (i.) the Alphabetic names and (ii.) the Syllabic names under the notes.

242. Write the above tune an octave lower in the Bass Clef.

243. Write the following—first in short score (as here) and afterwards in full vocal score.

244. Re-write the following passages showing by figures the position of the various beats, and grouping all quavers and semiquavers when they belong to the same beat. Section (*a*) is worked in full as an example.

(a) Question.

(a) Answer.

(b)

(c)

(d)

(e)

245. If the crotchet is value for a beat show how you would write notes of the following lengths, (*a*) two beats, (*b*) three beats, (*c*) two half-beat notes, (*d*) four quarter-beat notes, (*e*) one note of one and a half beats.

246. If three equal notes are to be sung to one beat (when crotchet = the beat) show how such notes should be written.

247. And again, if minim = the beat.

248. And again, if dotted crotchet = the beat.

249. Show by diagram or otherwise how you would beat time for a tune; (*a*) in 2/4 time, (*b*) in 3/4 time, (*c*) in quick 6/8 time, (*d*) in 4/4 time.

250. Add time signatures to the following and write at the beginning of each line the "beat" note.

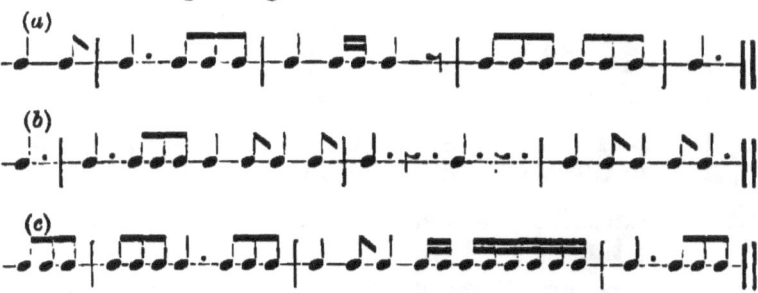

251. Re-write the exercises given in previous question, but taking the **crotchet** as the beat note in each case.

252. Re-write the following tune in $\frac{2}{4}$ time, preserving the relative accents:

253. Re-write the following tune in $\frac{6}{8}$ time, preserving the relative accents:

254. Write the following melody in Treble Clef in $\frac{4}{4}$ time:

C (leger line) minim, E crotchet, F and G quavers grouped.

A crotchet, F minim, E and D quavers grouped.

G crotchet, E minim, D and C quavers grouped.

D crotchet, D quaver, E and F semiquavers, E crotchet.

E quaver, F and G semiquavers, A quaver, C crotchet.

F quaver, E crotchet, D crotchet, C semibreve.

255. Point out the syncopated notes in the melody given in question 254.

256. Write the following melody in Bass Clef in ¼ time. (The figures denote fractions of a **beat**.) :

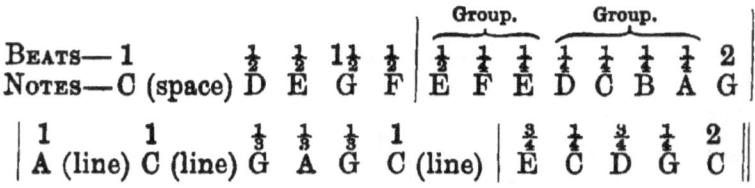

257. Transcribe the melody given in Question 256 into ⅔ time.

258. There are three instances of syncopation in the following melody. Write *a* over the example of a note continued from weak to strong accent; *b* over the note continued from weak to medium accent, and *c* over the note continued from last half of one beat to first half of next.

259. Similarly point out the syncopated notes in the following tune (by the use of *a*, *b* and *c*, as explained in previous question) :

260. Write the following melody in Treble Clef in 6/8 time. (The figures denote fractions of a **beat**—2 beats in a bar.) :

BEATS— 1 1 | 1 ⅓ ⅓ ⅓ | ⅔ ⅓ ⅔ ⅓ | 1 1 |
NOTES— G B | D (line) C B A | B G A F♯ | G rest |

| 1   1 ⅓ ⅓ 1 | ⅔ ⅔ ⅓ | 1   1 |
| E (space) D C D C B | A rest C♯ rest | D (line) D (space) |

| 1   1 | 1   1 ⅓ ⅔ ⅓ ⅔ | 2 ||
| E (line) G | D (space) G | E G F♯ A | G ||

261. Transcribe the melody given in previous question into ¾ time. (The figures will still denote fractions of a beat but the beat note will now be a crotchet instead of a dotted crotchet.)
262. What notes of the Scale bear Major Thirds and what bear Minor Thirds? (Read Art. 110.)
263. Show three Major Thirds in each of the following Keys:—C, G, D, A. [Do not use notes foreign to the signature.]
264. Show four Minor Thirds in the same Keys as in previous question.
265. Change each of the Minor Thirds mentioned in last question into a Major Third by the use of sharps or flats foreign to the signature.
266. Give the "typical examples" of Art. 116 in the Key of A♭ using the Bass Clef.
267. The Augmented Fourth is found on the Subdominant of a Major Key. Show this Interval in the Treble Clef in each of the following Keys:—F, B♭, E♭, A♭, D♭, G♭, C♭.
268. The Diminished Fifth is found on the leading note of a Major Key. Show this Interval in the Treble Clef in each of the Keys mentioned in previous question.
269. The Tonic of a Major Key always bears a Major Third. Show this Interval in the Treble Clef in each of the seven Keys, with sharps.
270. Give any four consecutive notes (a) of the ascending, and (b) of the descending Chromatic Scale.
271. Begin with the Tonic of Key E♭ Major (first line Treble Staff) and write a melody in semibreves, in accordance with the following directions:—
Major Second up; Minor Third down; Minor Second up; Major Third up; Perfect Fourth up; Major Second down; Minor Second down; Chromatic Semitone down; Minor Second down; Minor Third up; Perfect Fourth up; Perfect Fifth down; Major Third up; Minor Seventh down; Minor Second up.
[If you have interpreted the Intervals correctly your tune should end with the Tonic.]

272. Answer previous question in the Key of D Major.

273. Answer the same in E Major in Bass Clef.

274. Describe the following Intervals:—

275. Show each of the Intervals mentioned at the close of Chapter IV. in the Treble Clef and in the Key of B Minor.

276. Again show the same Intervals in the Bass Clef in the Key of G Minor.

277. Show the Interval of the Diminished Seventh in the Treble Clef in each of the following Keys:—A Minor, B Minor, C Minor, D Minor, E Minor, F Minor, G Minor.

278. Show the Augmented Second in the Bass Clef in each of the following Keys:—B♭ Minor, C♯ Minor, F♯ Minor, G♯ Minor.

279. On the sharpened Subdominant of each of the following Major Keys show the Interval of the Diminished Third. C, G, F, D, B♭.

280. Similarly on the flattened Submediant of the same Keys show the Interval of the Augmented Sixth.

281. State the Key of each of the following passages. Each passage is in one Key throughout.

282. Re-write each of the following in the Bass Clef an octave lower, giving the correct Key Signature—which is in every case different from the one given in question.

283. Re-write the following an octave higher in Treble Clef, giving correct Key Signatures.

284. There being only one Augmented Fourth in any Major Key, that Interval is sufficient of itself to determine the Key of any given Major Scale passage. Therefore determine the Key in each of the following examples.

285. What Major Key contains the following notes?
    a. F♯ G♯ C♯ and all the rest ♮.
    b. F♯ G♯ (C missing) and all the rest ♮.
    c. B♭ E♭ A♭ and all the rest ♮.
    d. E♭ A♭ (B missing) and all the rest ♮.
    e. Every note ♯.
    f. Every note ♭.

286. Taking la as the Tonic of a Minor Key (movable doh system) write the following in the Key of D Minor, adding the Key Signature.
    a. la ti do re mi fa sol la
    b. la ti do re mi fa♯ sol♯ la
    c. la ti do re mi fa sol♯ la

287. Similarly write the same three forms of the Minor Scales of G, F♯, F, and B Minor.

288. The Minor Scale contains alternative forms of the sixth and seventh degrees. Show these alternative notes in the Scales of A Minor, C Minor, C♯ Minor and E Minor.

289. Write the Scale of E Minor ascending and descending, using the Major Sixth and Major Seventh in the ascending portion of your scale, and the Minor Seventh and Minor Sixth in the descending portion.

290. Apply the previous question to the Scale of B Minor.

291. Write the Scale of G Minor ascending and descending, using the Minor Sixth and Major Seventh in the ascending portion, and the Minor Seventh and Minor Sixth in the descending portion.

292. Add the necessary sharps or flats **in front of** each of the following notes (and not as a Key Signature) so as to make the Harmonic Form of the Scale of C Minor.

293. Place in front of each note, where necessary, the sharp which will make this the Harmonic Form of the Scale of F♯ Minor.

294. Find the Key of each of the following passages, and then re-write, using the correct Key Signatures.

295. Pick out the Augmented Second, the Augmented Fifth, the Diminished Seventh, and the Diminished Fourth (where present) in each of the tunes given in previous question.

296. Transpose each of the tunes in question 294 a Major Second higher, using the correct Key Signatures.

297. Transpose the following tune into B♭ Minor, giving correct Key Signature.

298. Re-write the following tune in such a Key as to bring it well within the compass of an average class of school children (say Standard V.)

299. Transpose the following tune so that the highest note shall be E♭.

300. Compose a melody suitable for children in the Upper Standards and in it make use of four or five of the following musical terms and signs ; cres., dim., sf., |||, p., ff, < >, ⌢, rall., D.S., 𝄋, Fine.

INDEX.

The references are to the ARTICLES *in the text, not to the pages.*

	ART.
Accent	73
,, principal	75
,, secondary	75
,, sub-secondary	76
,, strong, medium, weak	77
Acciaccatura	169
Accidentals	140
,, when indicating modulation	153
Ad lib.	164
Ad libitum	164
Acute harmonics	182
Aliquot part	65
Al segno	165
Alto voice	28
,, C clef	31
Alphabetic names of notes	10
Appoggiatura	168
Attendant keys	149
Augmented intervals	120, 121
Auxiliary notes	169
Bass voice	6
,, clef	25
Bars	50
,, double	162, 163
Bar lines	50
Beats	51
Beating time	51
Beat, a grace note	169
Bind	47
Breve	44
C clef, alto	31
C clef, tenor	32
Chord	183
,, root of	184
,, inversion of	187

	ART.
Chord, first inversion of	187
,, second inversion of	188
,, six-four	188
,, six-three	187, 189
,, figured	187, 188, 189, 190
Chromatic intervals	125
,, semitones	125
,, scales	125
,, form of minor scale	133
Clef	21
,, treble, G clef	22
,, bass, F clef	25
,, alto, C clef	31
,, tenor, C clef	32
Common chord	184, 185
,, time	61
Compass of voices	41
,, of bass, tenor, alto, treble voices	41, 196
Compound intervals	157a
,, time	66, 67, 68, 72
Conjunct	184
Crescendo	173
Crotchet	44
Crushing note	199
Da capo	163
D.C.	163
Dal segno	165
Dashes	171
Decrescendo	173
Demisemiquaver	44
Diatonic interval	125
,, semitone	125
,, form of minor scale	131
Distant key	151
Diminuendo	173
Diminished intervals	122, 123
,, chord	185

		ART.
Dominant..		143
Dots		46, 171
Dotted notes		46
,, rests		48
Double-dotted notes		46
Double bar		162, 163
,, ,, with dots		163
,, octave		40
,, sharp		94
,, flat		95
Doubling..		159
Duple time		63, 65, 72
Duration..		42
Embellishments..		169
Enharmonic		153
Expression, terms relating to..		175
Extraneous modulation		151
Extremes of interval		107
F clef		25
First inversion of a chord		187
Figuring of chords		188, 189, 190
Fixed Do system		157a
Flat		95
,, double		95
,, sixth, or seventh		137
Flattening		191
Fundamental position		186
Full score		35
G clef		22
Grace notes		167
Great staff		14
Halving of notes		158
Harmonic form of minor scale		133, 142
Harmonics		182
Harmonies		181
Harmony		2
Hints on answering		41
How to tell minor key..		137a
In alt.		40
In altissimo		40
Interval		84, 107
,, kinds of		108
,, quality of		109, 110, 111
,, extremes of		107
,, value of		109

		ART.
Interval how to tell kind and quality of		117
,, how to form		118
,, major, and minor		109, 125
,, perfect,		111, 112, 113, 116, 125
,, augmented		120, 121
,, diminished		122, 123
,, diatonic		125
,, chromatic		125
,, in major scale		109 to 115
,, in minor scale		142
,, tables of		125
,, compound		157a
Inversion of intervals		176, 177
,, of chord		187
,, first		187
,, second		188
Key		100
,, note		101a
,, distant or remote		151
,, naming the		101a, 105a, 137a, 142a
Keys, relative or attendant		149
Key signatures—Tables of		101, 105
,, subordinate or secondary..		147
Keyboard, diagram of..		89
Leading note		132, 143
Leaning ,,		168
Leger lines		37
Lines		23
Major interval		109, 125, 127
,, mode		141
,, ,, character of		141
,, scale		127
,, ,, character of		141
,, common chord		185
,, triad		185
Measures		50
Mediant..		143
Medium accent		77
Melody		2
Mental effects		143
Metronome		78
,, description of		78
Middle C		19, 38, 39
Minim		44
Minor interval		109, 125, 127
,, mode		141
,, ,, character of		141

	ART.
Minor scale	127
,, ,, unaltered form	131
,, ,, harmonic or chromatic form	133
,, ,, melodic or altered diatonic form	134
,, ,, fourth form	134
,, ,, various examples of	134, 135, 136
,, ,, character of	141
,, ,, how to tell from signature	137a, 142a
,, ,, relative, how to write	131
,, ,, intervals found in	142
,, ,, tonic	142
,, common chord	185
,, triad	185
Mode	141
Modulation	144, 150
,, law of	146, 150
,, natural	151
,, extraneous	151, 152
,, enharmonic	153
Movable Do system	157a
Naming the key,	101a, 105a, 137a, 142a
Natural	96
,, modulation	151, 153
,, order of scale formation	97, 99, 145
Notes	8, 41
,, names of	10
,, grace	167
Octave	17
,, once marked, or one lined	40
,, two lined; three lined	40
,, double	40
Overtones	182
Principal accent	75
Pace, terms relating to	174
Pause	164
Perfect intervals	111, 116, 125
Pitch	33, 42
Prime	182
Quadruple time	63, 65, 72
Quaver	44
Questions on the text. See Contents.	

	ART.
Raised sixth	133, 134, 137
,, seventh	133, 134, 137
Registers	198, 199, 200
Relative keys	149, 150
,, minor scale	128, 129
,, ,, how to form	131
Remote key	151
Rests	48
,, dotted	48
Rhythm	73
Root of Chord	184
Scale	83
,, common	87, 88
,, major	106, 127
,, minor	106, 127
,, relative minor	128, 129, 138
,, tonic major	142
,, tonic minor	142
,, diatonic	106
,, chromatic	125
Scale formation, natural order of	97, 99
Score, full	35
,, short	36
Second inversion of a chord	188
Secondary accent	75
Secondary key	147
Semitone	84
Semibreve	44
Semiquaver	44
Semidemisemiquaver	44
Shape of time notes	43
Sharp	93
Sharp, double	94
Sharp seventh	137
,, interval	137
Short score	36
Signature, key, sharps	101
,, ,, flats	105
,, time	59
Simple time	65, 66, 72
Six-four chord	188
Six-three chord	187, 189
Slur	170
Sound	4
,, how produced	178
,, musical	10
Sounds, names of	10
Soprano	27
Spaces	23
Staccato	172
Staff	14, 16
,, great	14

	ART.
Staff, treble	16
,, bass	16
Strong accent	77
Style, terms relating to	175
Sub-dominant	143
Sub-mediant	143
Subordinate key	147
Super-tonic	143
Swell	173
Syllabic names of notes	10
Syncopation	81
Terms relating to pace	174
,, ,, expression	175
,, ,, style	175
Tenor voice	28
Tetrachord	86
Tie	47
Time	57
,, common	61
,, duple, quadruple, triple	63
,, signature	69
,, simple	65, 66
,, compound	66, 67
,, various kinds of	61 to 72
Tone	84
Tonic	142, 143
,, minor	142

	ART.
Tonic minor, forms of	142
,, major	142
Transcription	158
,, rules for	159
,, examples of	158 to 161
Transition	144
Transposition from one key to another	155, 156, 157
Transcription from one time to another	158, 159, 160, 161
Treble clef	22
,, voice	6, 27
Triad	184
,, inversions of	187, 188
Triple time	63, 65, 72
Triplet	82
Tritone	111
Unison	108
Value of beat, or bar	58
Value of interval	109, 116
Voices, kinds of	27, 28
Voice training	191 to 197
Weak accent	77

CATALOGUE

OF

Cusack's Series

of Text Books

IN

FREEHAND.	COPY BOOKS.
MODEL.	KINDERGARTEN DRAWING BOOKS.
SHADING.	
GEOMETRY.	ENGLISH LITERATURE.
ARITHMETIC.	PSYCHOLOGY AND LOGIC.
ALGEBRA.	NEEDLEWORK.
HISTORIES.	CUSACK'S JOURNAL.

Published by

CITY OF LONDON BOOK DEPOT,
WHITE STREET, MOORFIELDS,
LONDON, E.C.

BOOKS PUBLISHED BY PROFESSOR CUSACK.

Cusack's Series of Text Books, &c.,
FOR THE ELEMENTARY DRAWING CERTIFICATE.

CUSACK'S FREEHAND ORNAMENT.

Part I. Conventional Forms.—Including supplement containing Photographic Representations of Casts. 3/6 net, post free 3/11.

Cusack's Photographic Representations of Ornament, 30 plates, with analysis of each and instructions. 1/6 net, post free 1/8½.

By CHARLES ARMSTRONG, Late Art Master, City of London School of Art, Day Training College, Moorfields, London; Late of the National Art Training School. A complete course of instruction in Freehand Ornament, for all who are studying this subject for the Drawing Certificate. The book contains several hundred Exercises carefully graduated from the simplest curves up to the Examination Standard, with ample instruction in letterpress and explanatory diagrams.

Opinions of Experienced Practical Teachers.

"I consider Cusack's Freehand Ornament a very useful book, and remarkably cheap." J. T. COOK, *Art Master*, Sheffield School of Art.

"I can honestly recommend Cusack's Freehand Ornament as a book that all Art Teachers should have." H. BURROWS, *Art Master*, Huddersfield School of Art.

"It is the most complete book on Freehand Drawing I have seen." W. H. KNIGHT, *Art Master*, Northampton Technical School.

"It is a most valuable work, certainly the best of its kind that has yet come under my notice." JOHN FISHER, *Art Master*, Kensington School of Science and Art, Bristol.

"The designs are good and the methods of construction eminently suited for such pupils as are preparing for the Elementary Freehand Examination, and who are unable to obtain oral lessons. It should command a good sale as the price is very reasonable for so exhaustive a work." "ART MASTER."

"It is a thorough reliable work, and I should be pleased to see it in the hands of all my pupils." HENRY STOTT, *Art Master*, Bolton Municipal School of Art.

"It seems to me to be an excellent work, and treats the subject in a thorough and comprehensive manner. It should be of great assistance to students taking either the Elementary or Advanced stages of Freehand." FRANCIS REILY, *Art Master*, Southport Victoria Science and Art School.

"The book is full of very useful specimens suitable to the Elementary Student, and it is evidently the work of a practical teacher." BENJAMIN C. HASTWELL, *Art Master*, Charterhouse Art School, Goswell Road, E.C.

"The work is in book form, and is very suitable for those who wish to study Freehand privately, or to place in the hands of Pupil Teachers, &c. The examples are well chosen, and the method adopted to illustrate the construction cannot fail to produce better results. The directions at the beginning of the book are also very valuable, and I trust that the work will have a wide circulation." W. H. HEY, *Art Master*, Burnley School of Art, Lancashire.

"I consider Cusack's Freehand Ornament, by C. Armstrong, will be of great service to Teachers and Students." HAYWOOD RIDER, *Art Master*, Leeds School of Art.

"I have much pleasure in testifying to the great value of Cusack's Ornament. It certainly supplies a distinct want, and I am sure that if it is really studied and taken as a guide, much good will follow." R. B. DAWSON, *Art Master*, Rochdale School of Art.

BOOKS PUBLISHED BY PROFESSOR CUSACK.

CUSACK'S MODEL DRAWING.

3/6 net, post free 3/10.

BY THE SAME AUTHOR.

This book contains 200 explanatory diagrams and deals fully with many points never before attempted in a book on this subject, and but rarely even in classes. The letterpress is in each instance on the page opposite the diagrams to which it refers.

" A book for students, and one of the most complete and perfect guides to excellence in this branch of drawing that has come under our notice. The subject is dealt with in a most exhaustive manner, and every conceivable position in which the usual models can be placed is shown. We cordially recommend the work."—SCHOOLMISTRESS.

" Worthy of all praise.—Far ahead of anything we have yet seen."—SCHOOLMASTER.

" The result of several years' practical experience.—Well adapted to its purpose."—TEACHERS' AID.

" This is a splendid book, not only because it teaches model drawing on right lines, but because it teaches that *observation* and not mechanical rules must guide the student, and because it teaches what to observe and what to avoid.—We have never seen a more complete book than this one, whether for the elementary teacher or the student going in for his certificates."—ARNOLD'S ART CIRCULAR.

CUSACK'S SHADING

3/6 net, post free 3/10.

BY THE SAME AUTHOR.

This Book contains 20 finished plates, full examination size, and 60 explanatory diagrams. The descriptive letterpress is in each case on the page opposite the plate to which it refers, and on the same page as the explanatory diagrams. Methods of DRAWING THE CASTS, &c., to be shaded receive particular attention.

" This is a good practical work on a difficult subject, and calculated to help students."—SCIENCE AND ART.

" A very helpful text-book.—Two interesting plates show the different methods of obtaining the 'tones' in stump and in crayon respectively.—Progressive plates are given showing each new difficulty mastered before proceeding to something fresh. This work will be found especially valuable to all who are unable to attend art classes for direct instruction."—SCHOOLMASTER.

" This is a splendid book. We do not wonder to find that it is selling well. We can honestly recommend it. When seen it will recommend itself."—TEACHERS' AID.

" The best text-book on shading that has yet appeared."—ARNOLD'S ART CIRCULAR.

BOOKS PUBLISHED BY PROFESSOR CUSACK.

CUSACK'S HOW TO DRAW THE GEOMETRIC MODELS AND VASES.

9d. net, post free 10d. New Edition.

By A. A. BRADBURY, Art Master; Examiner in Art to the Science and Art Department.

"This is a practical little book on Model Drawing, alike instructive to the student and the teacher."—*Schoolmaster.*

"A few pence will put our readers in possession of one of the most valuable little aids it has ever been our lot to see."—*Schoolmistress.*

"Excellent little book."—*Science and Art.*

"Should be in the hands of every teacher."—*Board Teacher.*

"A most useful practical body of instruction."—*School Board Chronicle.*

"I think the idea of giving to each student a manual of instruction that contains the methods of construction he must practise to arrive at an accurate drawing, an excellent one. I hope the book may do all you have a right to expect from it." J. C. L. SPARKES,
Principal of the National Art Training School, South Kensington.

"Your work will, I trust, do much to correct the misapprehensions which are so prevalent in reference to Model Drawing."

J. A. D. CAMPBELL, Science and Art Department.

"I think highly of your little book. For shrewdness, brevity, and helpfulness, it is a model on its subject." M. SULLIVAN,
President of the Society of Art Masters.

"I have found your book exceedingly useful and a great help, especially to backward students."—J. VAUGHAN, *Art Master*, London Sch. Board.

"It is a model of conciseness and correct method of teaching. Send me one hundred copies."—J. T. COOK, *Head Master*, Sch. of Art, Sheffield.

"Your little book is full of valuable hints, and bids fair to become a very popular manual with all candidates for elementary or advanced model drawing. I wish it every success." HENRY R. BABB,
Head Master, Plymouth School of Art.

"I think the book is just what I require for my class."
CATHERINE F. MANNING, Diocesan Training Coll., Salisbury.

BOOKS PUBLISHED BY PROFESSOR CUSACK.

CUSACK'S SOLID GEOMETRY.

FOR SCIENCE SUBJECT I.

3/6 net, post free 3/10.

Being a complete exposition of this difficult subject as now required for the Elementary Drawing Certificate.

By HENRY F. ARMSTRONG, late Art Master, National Art Training School, late Lecturer in Solid Geometry and Perspective at the City of London School of Art, Day Training College, Moorfields, London. Now Professor of Art at the M'Gill University, Montreal.

Opinions of Experienced Practical Teachers.

"The student who now stumbles over that difficult portion, points, lines, and planes, must indeed be a dullard. Mr. Armstrong seems to have excelled in this stage particularly, and it is just here that that very useful box of models and planes called the 'Geometrikon,' issued in connection with this work, will be found very useful indeed. In this it was a brilliant idea to use transparent xylonite for auxiliary planes.

The plates and text are carefully and simply prepared, avoiding all complication, everything being easily understood."

ARTHUR SCHOFIELD, Leeds School of Art.

"I cannot speak too highly of the 'Geometrikon'; it is, I consider, the best thing of its kind I have seen."

J. T. COOK, School of Art, Sheffield.

"The book will be found of essential value to Architectural and Engineering Students. I consider it the best text book I have seen on the subject. The diagrams and Cards (The Geometrikon), showing the different planes in Solid Geometry, will be most helpful to students preparing for the Examination of the Science and Art Department."

H. BURROWS, *Art Master*, 47, West Parade, Huddersfield.

"I have carefully looked through Cusack's Solid Geometry and have decided to use it as a text book in this School. The 'Geometrikon' is a most useful addition to the book."

J. FISHER, *Art Master*, Science and Art School, Bristol.

"I am especially pleased with the 'Geometrikon,' which should greatly lessen, if not entirely remove, many of the difficulties which orthographic projection presents to beginners.

"'Cusack's Solid Geometry' and the 'Geometrikon' certainly form together a most thorough and interesting course of instruction."

G. BEDFORD, *Art Master*, School of Science and Art, Torquay.

"A student who consistently works through your book with the aid of this instrument cannot fail at the May examinations."

B. C. HASTWELL, *Art Master*, Charterhouse School of Art.

"I think your Solid Geometry and the Geometrikon are two *most useful* things, the latter especially supplying a long felt want."

JOS. HARRISON, *Head Master*, Municipal School of Art and Design, Waverley Street, Nottingham.

A STUDENT writes:—"I purchased Cusack's Solid Geometry in March; I studied it right through, giving all my Easter holidays to it. I was the only student at my centre who passed in Geometry."

Two STUDENTS write:—"We are the only two in this town who passed in Geometry; all the rest failed. We were the only two who used Cusack's Solid Geometry, and were it not for that most valuable book we should have failed also."

BOOKS PUBLISHED BY PROFESSOR CUSACK.

CUSACK'S PATENT GEOMETRIKON.

A BOX OF APPARATUS FOR SIMPLIFYING THE STUDY OF SOLID GEOMETRY.

3/6 net, post free 3/10.

The box contains:—2 mahogany planes connected by patent brass hinges, with spring, which keeps the planes at right angles to one another, so as to represent the vertical and horizontal planes of projection, but which also permits the vertical plane to fall backwards flat, so that both planes represent one flat sheet of paper, and the line between them represents the X Y line.

 1 large transparent xylonite plane.
 1 large opaque cardboard plane.
 14 diagrams from Solid Geometry Book, on paper suitable size to fit into the hinged planes for experimental purposes.
 22 auxiliary diagrams, either on transparent xylonite planes or cardboard opaque planes, as required.
 1 cardboard specially cut to fold into model of tetrahedron with adjustment showing height of tetrahedron and method of finding it.
 1 each small wooden cube, square prism and hexagonal prism.
 2 steel pins, bead-headed.

The whole is designed to illustrate all the essential principles of Science Subject 1, from the most elementary to the most abstruse.

CUSACK'S PHYSIOGRAPHY.

571 pp. 3s. 6d. net.

By S. W. DAVIES, Associate of the Royal School of Mines, Murchison Medallist and Prizeman, late Royal Exhibitioner, Senior Science Master, and Lecturer in Physiography at the Day Training College, Moorfields. Specially prepared to the Elementary Stage of the South Kensington Syllabus, and for Pupil Teachers, Scholarship Certificate Students (Men and Women).

"Cusack's Physiography is an excellent book, well up to date in scientific matter, and thoroughly suitable for P. Ts. I can strongly recommend it."
    T. H. KEMP, P.T. Classes, Merthyr Tydfil.

"Cusack's Physiography is an excellent book for Pupil Teachers, and other students who intend taking up the Elementary Stage of Physiography. It has the great merit of being extremely clear, and is easy to understand."
    A. H. EMMS, Norwich.

"I consider Cusack's Physiography to be a first-rate work."
    W. FURNEAUX, P.T. Centre, Peckham, S.E.

"It seems to be written in a thoroughly simple and masterly way."
    REV. J. P. FAUNTHORPE, Whitelands College, Chelsea.

"I consider Cusack's Physiography a most useful book, well arranged, and well suited to the needs of Advanced as well as Elementary Students, to whom I shall have pleasure in recommending it."
    JOHN T. DICKINSON, Central Schools, Peterborough.

"Cusack's Physiography is adapted to the requirements of the present Syllabus of Elementary Physiography, and I have no hesitation whatever in recommending the book, either to outside candidates for Elementary Physiography, or to Students in Training Colleges."
    F. S. BUCK, St. Hild's College, Durham.

BOOKS PUBLISHED BY PROFESSOR CUSACK.

CUSACK'S EDITION OF SCOTT'S
MARMION. Canto VI. 2/ net.
SECOND EDITION.

For Candidates, 1900.

Over 200 pages, with Illustrations of all the Heraldic, Architectural, and Military Terms used in the Poem.

POST FREE 2/2½.

CUSACK'S EDITION OF GOLDSMITH'S
THE TRAVELLER, 1/- net.
For First Year Pupil Teachers, 1900.

CUSACK'S EDITION OF COWPER'S
TASK. Book IV. 1/ net.
For Scholarship Candidates, December, 1899.

CUSACK'S EDITION OF POPE'S
ESSAY ON MAN. Epistle IV.
1/ net.
For Scholarship Candidates, December, 1899 and 1900.

For Pupil Teachers at their respective Examinations in 1900. With Lives of the Authors, Copious Notes and Explanations. Derivations of all important Words, with hints for parsing all the difficult words, and analysing the more difficult sentences, with articles on Figures of Speech, Metre, &c.

Kindly oblige by bringing this under the notice of all Pupil Teachers in your School, or with whom you are otherwise acquainted.

CUSACK'S
REIGN OF QUEEN ELIZABETH.
For Scholarship Examination, December, 1899. **1/6 net.**

CUSACK'S TONIC SOL-FA MUSIC QUESTIONS
And How to Answer Them. **1/- net.**

BOOKS PUBLISHED BY PROFESSOR CUSACK.

CUSACK'S COPY BOOKS.
Adopted by the School Board for London.

Complete Series in 8 Nos., 1d. and 2d. each. Over 5,000 Schools and many of the Training Colleges now use them.

Set of Cusack's Copy Books for Teachers' Use, in one volume, 1/6 (cloth)

What Her Majesty's Inspectors say of them:—"We are everywhere meeting with Cusack's Copy Books now, and always with a marked improvement in the Handwriting." "The Handwriting is in style perfect; it combines every excellence." "I am very pleased to see the increased use of your excellent Copy Books in the schools that I visit."

What Head Teachers say of them:—"They are all that can be desired." "The children adopt the style most readily." "The Handwriting of my school has vastly improved since their introduction." "I feel compelled to write and tell you how excellent I find them." "Every school in this town now uses your Copy Books in every department, and the improvement is most remarkable." "I have used your Copy Books with marked success."

What the Press says of them:—"We have seen no better."—SCHOOLMASTER.

"A capital series, worthy of the attention of Teachers. The style of writing is bold, neat, and taking. No. 8 especially so."—TEACHERS' AID.

"The system is simple, most carefully graduated, and results in a style of writing so beautifully legible and yet sufficiently free, that a lad on leaving school can at once take his place at the merchant's desk with nothing in his handwriting either to learn or unlearn."—TEACHERS' MONTHLY.

"We strongly advise Teachers, who are on the look out for a thoroughly good and practical series of Copy Books, to obtain specimens of this admirable series before making their choice."—SCHOLASTIC GLOBE.

CUSACK'S WRITING BOOKS (Blank).
For Blackboard Lessons.
RULED TO MATCH CUSACK'S COPY BOOKS.   1d. each.

CUSACK'S SELECTED PENS.
In 5 grades—Nos. 1 to 5—to suit writing of every size.

No. 1.—A Superior Pen for Commercial Work, or for large hand in Schools.
No. 2.—A Superior Pen for General Correspondence or for text hand in Schools.
No. 3.—A Superior strong hard-pointed Pen, for rapid writing.
No. 4.—A Superior fine hard-pointed Pen, very suitable for ledger work.
   Nos. 3 and 4 are suitable for small hand in Schools.
No. 5.—A Superior Mapping Pen.

Each Pen has been carefully tested by hand before being packed, so that they will be found of uniform quality. They are guaranteed to be of the finest quality, and of great durability, being made of the finest Damascus Steel.

Specimens free to Teachers. Packed only in One Gross Boxes.

Prices :—Nos. 1 & 2, **2/-** net, per gross. Nos. 3, 4 & 5, **2/6** net per gross.

Sample Box of Assorted Pens, 6d., or 2 doz. of any one number, 6d.

CUSACK'S SELECTED PENHOLDERS.
3/- net, per gross.

BOOKS PUBLISHED BY PROFESSOR CUSACK.

FOR CERTIFICATE STUDENTS—JULY, 1900.

CUSACK'S
HISTORICAL GEOGRAPHY OF EUROPE.
1700 to 1789.

By P. W. RYDE, F.R.G.S.

Price 2/ net, post free 2/2½.

Every Student should be provided with a copy. It deals very fully with History, General Aspect, Trade, Industries, Politics, Religion, and Social Standing of each Country, and contains copious fully coloured maps.

CUSACK'S JOURNAL.

A Monthly Newspaper for Pupil Teachers, Acting Teachers, and all Teachers.

Containing much instructing and educative matter. All current topics dealt with. Published 15th of each month, price 1d.; by post, 1½d., of all newsagents and stationers.

CUSACK'S LEAD PENCIL COPY BOOKS
FOR INFANT SCHOOLS.

Complete Series in 4 Books. Price 8d. per dozen net.

The objections to slates and slate pencils are many:—

1. It is impossible to hold the slate pencil as the pen *should be held* in writing; hence infants contract bad habits, difficult to eradicate afterwards.
2. The noise of the pencil on the slate is unpleasant, and irritating to many.
3. As the copies are all rubbed out, there can be no permanent record of the child's work or progress.
4. The means adopted in many cases for cleaning the slate is an effective cause of the spread of infectious diseases among children.

These and many other objections are at once obviated by the use of Paper and Lead Pencil.

In the above series of Copy Books, besides the Headlines being given in a bold style, the whole page is outlined with the given copy.

The very low price quoted, **only Eightpence per dozen,** *should bring them within the reach of all Schools.*

Specimen set (free) will be sent to the Head Teacher of any Infant School.

CUSACK'S BRITISH MADE LEAD PENCILS, 8/. NET PER GROSS.
EVERY PENCIL SHARPENED.

BOOKS PUBLISHED BY PROFESSOR CUSACK.

CUSACK'S ALGEBRA,

PART I. (ELEMENTARY), 2/6 net, post free 2/9.

Written expressly for

Scholarship Candidates (Girls), and for Second Year Women Certificate Students.

Adopted by the Chief Pupil Teachers' Centres, Training Colleges, &c.

OPINIONS OF EXPERIENCED PRACTICAL TEACHERS.

"The feature of the book is the remarkable fulness of the explanatory matter, making a demonstration on the Blackboard by a teacher quite unnecessary—a good thing for rural teachers who cannot attend a class in Mathematics."

G. M. HANDLEY, Head Master, Oldham P. T. Central Classes.

"Cusack's Algebra is an Excellent Book. Considering the class of Students for whom it is intended, it is without a rival."

JOHN FARISH ROBY, P.'T. Centre, Manchester.

"This is an excellent text book, admirably suited for its special purpose, and evidently written by a practical teacher of wide experience."

G. J. RANKILOR, Director, Church P. T. Central Classes, Birmingham.

"It is a good book and very carefully graduated."

W. DONE, Supt. P. T. School, Brighton and Preston, Sussex.

"A great help to private students."

Mr. CANHAM, Mathematical Master, P. T. Centre, Norwich.

OPINIONS OF STUDENTS.

"I am a student in a Scholarship Class, I procured your Algebra at the beginning, and I must say that I think it excellent. I have never attempted that subject before, and I was looking forward to its commencement with a dread of all the hard work it would entail. But I am pleased to say that I have taken a great interest in it, and enjoy its perusal exceedingly."

LOUIE ARTHUR, St. Peter's Park.

CUSACK'S ALGEBRA.

Part II. Advanced.

For Scholarship Candidates (Boys) and Certificate Students (Men), both First and Second Year. 3/6 net, post free 3/10.

Specially prepared for those Students who have not the opportunity of attending Oral Classes. Dealing very fully in Evolution, Theory of Indices, Surds, Quadratic Equations, Equations Involving Surds, Factors, Propositions, Ratio, Proportion, Variation, Progression, Logarithms, Binomial Theorem, &c.

CUSACK'S REIGN OF GEORGE III. 3/6 net.

BOOKS PUBLISHED BY PROFESSOR CUSACK.

CUSACK'S MENSURATION.

For Pupil Teachers, Scholarship Candidates (Boys) and Certificate Students (Men), both First and Second Year. By H. J. SMITH, B.Sc., Lecturer in Mathematics at the Day Training College, Moorfields, London, E.C.—2s. 6d. net, post free 2/9.

" We have long wanted a new book on this subject; the examples in the old ones are worn out. I endorse the remarks of Mr. H. J. Smith in his preface."
W. DONE, Supt. P. T.'s School, Brighton.

"This book is undoubtedly one of the best published. The explanations are simple and clear, and the numerous worked examples exhibit a style well worthy of imitation. The proofs of rules are especially good, and exactly meet the requirements of Certificate and Scholarship students."
G. J. RANKILOR, Director Church P. T. Central Classes, Birmingham.

" 1. Many good examples worked out.   4. Proofs simply explained.
2. Exercises good and plentiful.   5. Diagrams very clear.
3. Short cuts plainly indicated.   6. Difficulties anticipated."
H. W. DUFFIN, P. T.'s School, Norwich.

CUSACK'S ELEMENTS OF LOGIC.

NEW EDITION, Published on Nov. 1st, 1899.

Prepared expressly to meet the requirements of Syllabus for 2nd year Certificate Students. By S. BLOWS, M.A., Hons. Cantab., B.A., Hons. B.Sc., and Teacher's Diploma, London.—2/6 net, post free 2/9.

CUSACK'S ELEMENTS OF PSYCHOLOGY.

By S. BLOWS, M.A.—2s. net, post free 2s. 3d.

CUSACK'S LECTURES ON MUSIC.

Staff Notation.

2nd Edition.   2/- net, post free 2/3.

This book comprises all the requirements in Staff Notation for Pupil Teachers of all years, Scholarship Candidates, and Certificate Students of both First and Second year.

It deals very fully with Clefs, Minor Scales, Intervals, Modulation, Transposition from one Scale to another, and from one time to another, and with the Metronome in a manner never before attempted in any text book on the subject.

"The work is to be commended for its rugged outspoken style, and its terseness."—SCHOOLMASTER.

" The Lectures are thoroughly practical—Ought to prove useful to our readers."—TEACHERS' AID.

"We have gone through the book carefully, and can give it high praise."—
SCHOLASTIC GLOBE.

"An excellent and highly recommendable little work. For cogency of style and clearness of expression the book is admirable, evidencing unmistakably the wide experience of the author in imparting instruction. The book is calculated to prove of much service to the Student, from the clearness and force of its style, and the thoroughness and earnestness with which the various subjects are put before the tyro."—KEYBOARD.

BOOKS PUBLISHED BY PROFESSOR CUSACK.

NEEDLEWORK FOR STUDENT TEACHERS.

By AMY K. SMITH, Diplomée of the London Institute for the Advancement of Plain Needlework. Specialist at the Day Training College, Moorfields, E.C. With an introduction by the Lady WOLVERTON. 3/6 net, post free 3/10. 4th Edition.

NEEDLEWORK DIAGRAMS.

By Miss A. K. SMITH.

Specially prepared for Scholarship and Certificate Candidates.

Scholarship, 1/- net.   First Year Women, 1/- net.

Second Year Women, 1/- net.

We strongly advise all Students troubled about the "Needlework requirements," to invest 1/ in the purchase of a set of papers on the subject by Miss A. K. SMITH. These papers are excellent in every way.

TEACHERS' AID.

CUSACK'S ARITHMETIC.

For Pupil Teachers, Scholarship Candidates, and Certificate Students, Men and Women. 4s. 6d. net, post free 4s. 10d. Second Edition.

"If it were possible for a book to supersede personal teaching, this book would make a teacher superfluous. We have here a full, clear, concise and amply illustrated exposition of the theory, and a well-selected list of graded exercises embodying every conceivable form of problem. The usual catch questions—train and clock sums, &c., are explained with the aid of diagrams (trains, clocks, &c.), with such clearness that one cannot conceive of an ordinary private student failing to work even abstruse problems. It is the best work of Arithmetic that we have seen."

PUPIL TEACHER AND SCHOLARSHIP STUDENT.

"No pains seem to have been grudged to make the whole book thoroughly serviceable, and after a careful examination, we have nothing for it but words of commendation. Many pages read like actual demonstrative lectures, with all the mark of a strong personality in the lecturer."—PRACTICAL TEACHER.

"It is, in our opinion, one of the most complete and educative treatises on the subject yet published."—SCHOOLMISTRESS.

CUSACK'S KINDERGARTEN DRAWING COPY BOOKS.

Complete Series in 8 Nos., 2d. nett.

A preparation for Frœbel's Drawing.

Designed and arranged by C. PATTISON, A.F.S.

Specimen pages post free on application.

CUSACK'S
KINDERGARTEN DRAWING EXERCISE BOOK, 4½d. NETT.

Interleaved with tissue. Specially prepared for drawing Kindergarten Diagrams, and for Students' use.

BOOKS PUBLISHED BY PROFESSOR CUSACK.

CUSACK'S ATLAS OF THE BRITISH EMPIRE.

For Scholarship Candidates, Dec., 1899, 1/- net, post free 1 2.

CUSACK'S ATLAS OF EUROPE.

1/- net., post free, 1/2.

For Certificate Candidates, July, 1900.

CUSACK'S MAP DRAWING.

Specially prepared for Pupil Teachers, Scholarship Candidates and Certificate Students, both 1st and 2nd year, so as to enable them to produce Memory Maps neatly and quickly in the Examination Room. By P. W. RYDE, F.R.G.S., Lecturer in Geography at the Day Training College, Moorfields, London, E.C. 2/ net, post free 2/3. 3rd Edition.

CUSACK'S REPRINTS OF SCHOLARSHIP QUESTIONS.

10 years—1888–1897. All subjects classified.—2/ net, post free 2/2.

CUSACK'S REPRINTS OF CERTIFICATE ARITHMETIC.

10 years—1888–1897. 1/ net, post free 1/1.

CUSACK'S EDITION OF "GRAY'S ELEGY."

Price 1s. net.

CUSACK'S SHORTHAND NOTE BOOK,

200 pp., 4½d. net, Post Free 7d.

BOOKS PUBLISHED BY PROFESSOR CUSACK.

CUSACK'S OBJECT LESSONS.

By LOUISA WALKER,

Head Mistress of Fleet Road Board School, Hampstead,
(Infants' Department).

Part I.—2/ net, post free 2/3.

Part II.—2/6 net, post free 2/9.

CONTENTS OF PART I—.

ANIMAL WORLD.

Bat — Bear — Beaver — Bees — Butterfly — Camel — Cat — Codfish — Cow—Cuckoo—Dog—Duck—Eagle—Elephant—Frog—Giraffe—Goat—Hedgehog—House Fly—Horse—Lion—Mole—Monkey—Ostrich—Pig—Polar Bear—Rabbit—Reindeer—Robin—Seal — Sheep — Silk and the Silkworms—Spider—Squirrel—Swallow and the Whale.

CONTENTS OF PART II—

MINERAL AND VEGETABLE WORLD
AND
COMMON OBJECTS.

Apple — Bone — Butter—Buttercup—Candles—Chalk—Coal—Cocoa-nut—Coffee—Coins in Use—Copper—Cork—Corn—Cotton—Cup and Saucer — Earthenware — Egg—Feather—Flax—Fruit—Fur—Glass—Gold—Gutta-percha—Honey and Wax—Horn—India-rubber—Iron—Ivory—Knife and Fork (Parts)—Knife and Fork (Manufacture)—Lead—Leather—Leaves—Milk—Needle (Parts)—Needle (Manufacture)—Orange—Paper—Penny—Potato — Pins — Salt — Silk — Silver — Slate—Soap—Sponge—Sugar—Tea—Tin—Tree (Parts)—Wood—Wool—Zinc.

BOOKS PUBLISHED BY PROFESSOR CUSACK.

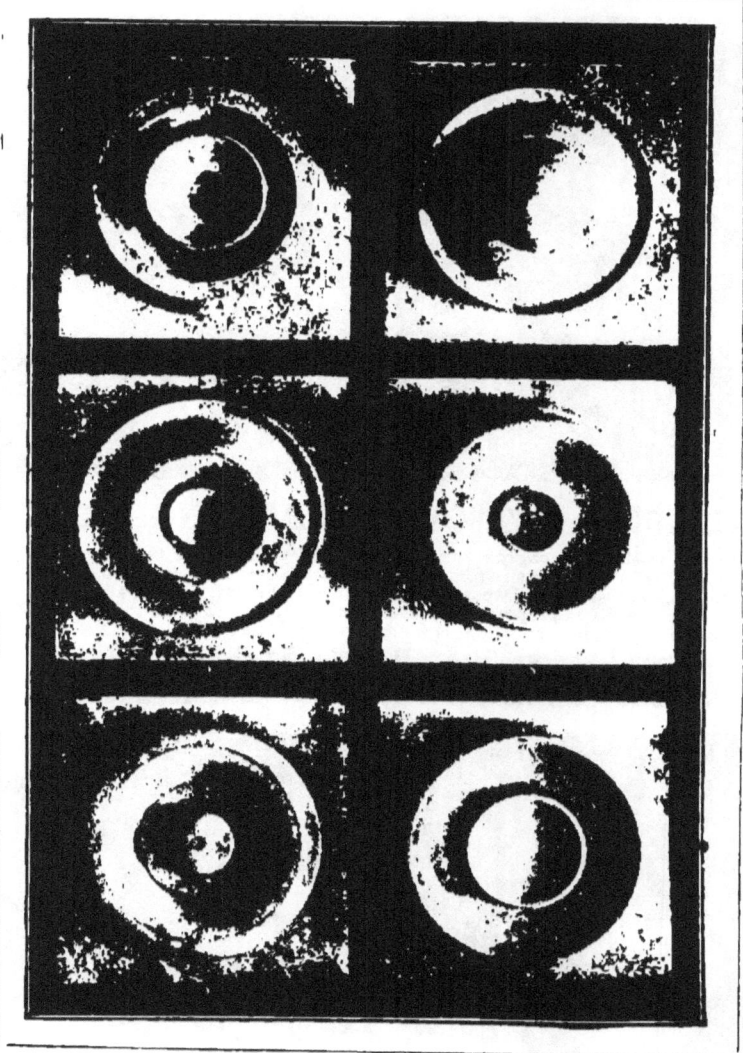

From a photograph of the set of casts.

CASTS FOR SHADING.

Cusack's Set of Six Elementary Rosette Forms
(In Wood) afford the best possible practice for beginners in Shading.
In 1898 the Examination in Elementary Shading was based on a rosette.
Price 10/6 net, Carriage Paid.   Packing Cases and Packing Free.

BOOKS PUBLISHED BY PROFESSOR CUSACK.

CUSACK'S SET OF 10 DRAWING MODELS.

' Perfect in shape, strongly made in wood; and painted. In two sizes: Large and Small. The large is the size for Schools of Art and Art Classes. The size prescribed by the Science and Art Department for the May Exams. Large size: cube 10 in., and other models in proportion, as shown in diagram. The small size (cube 6½ in., and other models in proportion) is for students' private study.

Prices—Large Size, 40/- net; Small Size, 20/- net.
Carriage paid. Packing Case and Packing Free.

CUSACK'S SET OF 4 MODELS.

Sphere, Skeleton Cube, Small Cube, Vase. In Wood. Price 16/- net
Carriage Paid and Packing Free.
In two sizes: Large Size, 16/- net; Small size, 8/- net.

www.ingramcontent.com/pod-product-compliance
Lightning Source LLC
Chambersburg PA
CBHW031829230426
43669CB00009B/1276